Portraits
of Christ
in
Genesis

Portraits of Christ in Genesis

M. R. DeHAAN, M.D.

Lamplighter
Books
Grand Rapids,
Michigan
Zondervan Publishing House

FOREWORD

Last words are precious words!

Last words are held in fondest esteem!

How we cherish the memories of departed loved ones, and all that they have said and done — and yet, how much more impressive, how much more meaningful and significant are their final words.

For that reason, this particular book is most deeply treasured. It contains my father's *last written words*. During his final months with us, although extremely weak and tiring at the least bit of effort, the burden of his heart was that he might complete this volume — to share with others these studies which had brought such rich blessing to him. The Lord supplied the strength, gave the days, and granted his desire. But, this was to be his last work, his twenty-fifth volume.

Having fought a good fight, having finished his course, having kept the faith, he was ushered into the presence of his Lord on December 13, 1965. How thankful I am, however, that although his strong voice has been silenced and his pen laid to rest, through this volume he "being dead yet speaketh," and his "works do follow."

RICHARD W. DE HAAN
Radio Bible Class, Inc.
Grand Rapids, Michigan

INTRODUCTION

"Of making many books there is no end; and much study is a weariness of the flesh" (Ecclesiastes 12:12). When many months ago I began to give consideration to an extended series of messages to be given over the air, and subsequently also to be printed in a clothbound volume, it was not an easy matter to decide upon a subject. Not too long ago I had already given a series of messages based on the Book of Genesis, and I had serious doubts as to the wisdom of issuing another volume which would cover very largely the same book. However, the subject matter being so much different, I finally decided that it would be profitable in these days in which we are living.

At first the publication of a book entitled "Portraits of Christ" was intended to be a study of portraits of Christ in the entire Bible. However, as I began to collect material, I realized what a hopeless task I was undertaking and so I next limited it to portraits of Christ in the Old Testament. Again, I had not gone very far when I realized that this too was a Herculean task which could hardly be done in one volume, or even many volumes. As a result, it was shortened to "Portraits of Christ in the Pentateuch," the books of Moses. Then, finally, after completing but one chapter, I realized that I could not even begin to discuss thoroughly the portraits of Christ in the first book of the Bible alone, the Book of Genesis. After many years of Bible study, I was amazed at the volume of material and subject matter in the Book of Genesis alone, which was the revelation of the Lord Jesus Christ. The last book of the Bible opens with "the revelation of Jesus Christ," and this may well be taken to be the title of the entire Bible, from the very first verse of Genesis, chapter 1, until the close of the Book of the Revelation. It is one continuous, progressive revelation concerning the Altogether Lovely One, the Son of God, and the Son of Man.

There was, however, another reason for limiting our study to the Book of Genesis, and this is because of the rapidly mounting attacks upon this particular part of the Word of God. The books of Moses have long been the target for the higher critics and the infidels of the ages past, but just recently there seems to have been a renewal of concerted effort to discredit the first book of the Bible. There is a veritable deluge of material coming off the presses today which seems to discredit the historical, literal account of creation, the origin of man, the historicity of the Flood, and other matters discussed in the Book of Genesis. New curriculums have been set up which take as their basic principle that the Book of Genesis, if not all the books of Moses, is largely mythological, and belongs in a class with fairy tales and fables. Because of this shocking trend, we felt that a re-emphasis on the inspiration and authenticity of the Book of Genesis might be in order. This is not written in any sense as a defense, nor as a proof of the inspiration of the Book of Genesis, for we trust you will see from these chapters that it needs no proof, and needs no defense, but needs only to be preached, and to be presented. The evidence is so overwhelming, that to the spiritually enlightened mind there is no question whatsoever concerning the authenticity, and the authority, and the historicity of the five books of Moses. This is particularly true of the Book of Genesis.

This volume is therefore not written to convince the unregenerate mind of the genuineness of the Word of God, but

Introduction

rather to present the Word in such a way that the Holy Spirit may enlighten the mind of the unregenerate, causing spiritual eyes to be opened to see without argument or discussion the overwhelming evidence of the inspiration of the Word of God. We have been able in this volume to treat only a very few of the outstanding and unmistakable types and figures and shadows of the Lord Jesus Christ in the Book of Genesis, and we trust that this will merely whet the appetite of the reader to investigate for himself, and delve more deeply into this inexhaustible mine of revelation concerning the Creator of the Universe, the Word of God.

CONTENTS

Foreword

Introduction

1

CHRIST IN CREATION

The Bible is a picture Book with descriptive portraits on practically every page. I realize that this may be an entirely new view of the Bible, yet it is true. To be sure, the Bible is not illustrated with visual pictures and drawings, but it nevertheless is a Book of pictures. There are two kinds of pictures: first, those drawn by pen, pencil, or brush, or those taken by photography, which are visual; that is, they can be seen by the physical eye. In addition to these, there are also mental pictures or images drawn on the canvas of the mind and memory which are word pictures, either seen or heard. We hear someone graphically describe some scene or incident or occurrence in words, and there is painted upon the scroll of our mind a mental image or picture of the incident, although neither pen, pencil, crayon, nor brush has been employed. These are *word* pictures which are as clearly seen and remembered as though we beheld them by the physical eye as visible illustrations or drawings.

Bible Full of Pictures

The Bible is a Book of such pictures and portraits. Although it contains no visual picture or portrait in the generally accepted sense of the word, it is filled with *word* pictures, and all these have as their central figure a Person, and that Person is the Lord Jesus Christ, the Son of God and

Son of Man, the Saviour of sinners. If we search long enough we shall find upon every page of Scripture, standing somewhere in the shadow, the outline of the central Person of the Book — the Lord Jesus Christ, both the object and end of all Scripture. The last book of the Bible opens with the words, "The Revelation of Jesus Christ," and this is not only the title of the last book of the Bible, but it may well be taken as the title of all the books of the Bible, for it is truly the "revelation of Jesus Christ." Every incident recorded in the Scriptures has a bearing directly or indirectly upon this theme, "revealing Jesus Christ." A godly minister, now gone to be with the Lord, said to me early in my ministry, "Son, you have never found the true interpretation of any passage of the Scriptures until you have found in it somewhere a reference to the Lord Jesus Christ. If you search long enough you will find Him standing somewhere in the background, sometimes clear and unmistakable, sometimes faintly and dimly, but He is there."

I have never forgotten that bit of advice and it has been of untold help to me. Jesus Christ is the theme and the subject of every part of the Scriptures. Jesus Himself made this claim when He said in John 5 to those who questioned His authority:

> Search the scriptures; for in them ye think ye have eternal life: and *they are they which testify of me* (John 5:39).

And again in John 5 we read:

> Do not think that I will accuse you to the Father: there is one that accuseth you, even Moses, in whom ye trust.
> For had ye believed Moses, ye would have believed me: *for he wrote of me* (John 5:45, 46).

JESUS IN ALL THE BIBLE

Jesus Himself asserted that the Bible was the *revelation of Himself*. This He once more asserted after His Resurrection, when, walking with the two disciples on the road to Emmaus He said to them:

> . . . O fools, and slow of heart to believe *all* that the prophets have spoken;
> And beginning at Moses and *all the prophets,* he expounded unto them in *all the scriptures* the things concerning himself (Luke 24:25, 27).

We might multiply passages to show that not only Jesus Himself made this claim, but also the writers (the human authors) of the Scriptures assert beyond doubt the fact that the Bible is indeed the *revelation of Jesus Christ, the Son of God.* With this basic fact in mind, we begin our study of *Portraits of Christ in Genesis.* We remind you again, these are *word* pictures, and they are found throughout the entire Bible from the opening chapter of Genesis to the closing verse of the book of the Revelation of Jesus Christ.

Attack Upon the Word

If we but remember that the Bible is the *revelation* — the unveiling — of Jesus Christ, and the only pictures we have of Him are the *word* pictures of the Bible, we can understand the reason for Satan's attack upon the Scriptures. It is really an attack upon Jesus Christ, veiled as a critical examination of the *Word* which tells us about Him. Satan's attack upon the *Word* of God began way back in the Garden of Eden when he said to the woman, "Yea, hath God said?" (Genesis 3:1). His first and initial attack upon Jesus Christ was disguised as an innocent request for information. He asked the woman, "Just what did God mean when He said, 'Ye shall not eat of every tree of the garden?'" It seemed like an innocent inquiry for additional information. It sounded so innocent, but underneath it was a subtle attempt to corrupt and discredit the Word of God. Poor, unsuspecting Eve fell for the clever ruse, and in apparent good faith (not knowing the adversary's cunning scheme) she gave her own version of what God had said to her husband Adam.

Satan Has Not Changed

After six thousand years of human history, Satan's strategy has not been altered or changed. It worked so perfectly the first time he tried it that he has not deviated from the original plan since, but today is using the very same tactics. Under the guise of a search for knowledge and better understanding of the Word of God, the enemies of the Gospel are repeating the question of the serpent, "Yea, hath God said?" Just how must we interpret the Word of God? Must we accept it as a literal account, or is it merely an allegory? Are the books of Moses, and especially the Book of Genesis, a literal account of the creation of the world and the creation of animals and man, or is it only a valuable set of myths and fairy tales? The question once more is, "Yea, hath God said?" Are we to take the Word of God literally, or can we spiritualize it and accept it because it teaches valuable ethical and moral lessons, while rejecting it as a literal, historical account? In short, is the story of creation on a level with the fable of Pandora's box, and other pagan records of creation?

This attack upon the veracity of the historical account of creation as given in Genesis, even though disguised as a sincere search for truth, is more than an attempt to discredit the *written* record, it is in reality an undermining of the *incarnate Word of God*, the Lord Jesus Christ Himself. If the record of the five books of Moses, as well as the rest of Scripture, is not fact, then Jesus Christ becomes either a deliberate imposter, or an ignorant fool. Now if you consider that a startling statement, then consider these facts.

Jesus Believed Moses' Writings

Do you know that Jesus Christ while here on earth quoted from all the five books of Moses? Do you know He placed His endorsement upon the authority and historicity of the Books of Genesis, Exodus, Leviticus, Numbers and Deuteronomy? Bear with me patiently while I elaborate this basic, important fact. Jesus believed the historical account of the creation of man in Genesis. When the Pharisees came to Jesus in Matthew 19, they asked Him the question:

> . . . It is lawful for a man to put away his wife for every cause? (Matthew 19:3).

Do you know how Jesus answered this question? By quoting from the second chapter of Genesis. He said:

> . . . Have ye not read, that he which made them at the beginning made them male and female,
> And said, For this cause shall a man leave father and mother, and shall cleave to his wife: and they twain shall be one flesh? (Mathew 19:4, 5).

This is a literal, word-for-word quotation of Genesis 2:23 and 24. Did Jesus believe the story of the creation of man? Did Jesus believe the literal account of the first chapters of Genesis? Do you see what these higher critics, skeptics, and unbelievers are doing when they try to make us believe the first few chapters of Genesis are mythology and fables? They are trying underhandedly to make a "monkey" of Jesus Christ Himself. Yes, Jesus believed the record of Genesis.

How About Exodus?

Did Jesus believe the record of the second book of the Bible — Exodus? He certainly did, and asserted it in no uncertain terms. Hear Him in Mark 12 or Luke 20. The Sadducees had come to Jesus with a catch question concerning a woman who had been married seven times, and they wanted to know whom she would claim as her husband in the resurrection (Mark 12:18-25). Do you remember how Jesus answered them? By referring them to Exodus 3, and the burning bush. He said to them:

> . . . have ye not read in the book of Moses, how in the bush [the burning bush of Exodus 3] God spake unto him, saying, I am the God of Abraham, and the God of Isaac, and the God of Jacob?

> He is not the God of the dead, but the God of the
> living . . . (Mark 12:26, 27).

Did Jesus believe that the story of the burning bush was
a fairy tale? He certainly did not, but accepted it as a literal
fact. The same is true of the Book of Leviticus. In Matthew
8 a leper came to Jesus, worshiping and praying to be healed.
After Jesus had stretched forth His hand to heal him, He
sent him to the priest and quoted the Book of Leviticus as
His authority. We read:

> And Jesus saith unto him, . . . go thy way, shew thy-
> self to the priest, and offer the gift that Moses com-
> manded, for a testimony unto them (Matthew 8:4).

This was a direct reference to Leviticus 14, where detailed
instructions are set forth for the cleansing of a leper. Did
Jesus believe the literal record of Leviticus? He certainly
did, and those who would tell us that these books of Moses
are not authentic are backhandedly calling Jesus either a
fool, an imposter or a liar.

How About Numbers?

It seems hardly necessary to show that Jesus believed the
historical record of Numbers and Deuteronomy. His reference in John 3 to the brazen serpent in the wilderness is too
well known to need any emphasis. Jesus in speaking to Nicodemus by night says,

> And as Moses lifted up the serpent in the wilderness,
> even so must the Son of man be lifted up:
> That whosoever believeth in him should not perish,
> but have eternal life (John 3:14, 15).

Jesus did not believe that the story of the brazen serpent
was a myth and a fable. If the record of the brazen serpent
be a myth, then the cross of Christ is a myth also. He links
the two inseparably together. And so we might go on with
Deuteronomy, and the rest of the Old Testament. In John 8

the Pharisees brought a woman caught in adultery, and quoted the penalty the law prescribed — even death. Yes, Jesus believed in the literal account of the books of Moses, and staked His own authority and reputation upon it. Listen to Him as He says in John's record:

> Do not think that I will accuse you to the Father: there is one that accuseth you, even *Moses* in whom ye trust.
> For had ye believed Moses, ye would have believed me: for he wrote of me (John 5:45, 46).

We remind you once again that Satan's first attempt at deceiving man was an apparently innocent and sincere question concerning just what God meant by what He plainly had spoken. But behind this cleverly concealed interest was a plan to cast doubt upon the plain, literal, unmistakable meaning of *thus saith the Lord*. Be on guard against any tampering with the Word, whether disguised as a search for truth, or a scholarly attempt at apparently hidden meanings; and beware of the confusion created by the senseless rash of new versions, translations, editions, and improvements upon the tried and tested Bible of our fathers and grandfathers.

And if you are unsaved, you need only to believe the simple message of (1) sin, (2) the Saviour, and (3) salvation. First, you must admit you are a sinner. Then, that you cannot save yourself, and therefore you need a Saviour. Then, by accepting Him, "thou shalt be saved." There need be no misunderstanding concerning these three things: your sin, your Saviour, and your salvation.

2

CHRIST THE LIVING WORD

Do you remember the old family album with its record of old-fashioned pictures of the members of the family? It was a heavy volume filled with pictures of grandpa and grandma (probably tintypes), and then pictures of yourself when you were just a baby, a young girl or lad, or pictures of the wedding, etc. Instead of watching television we used to look over these ancient photographs and recall the many happy moments suggested by the various occasions on which the pictures were taken with our primitive cameras. The Bible is much like that old family album with its history written in a succession of pictures and photographs. This Bible Album contains many snapshots, but the one Person who appears in almost every scene is the eternal, never-aging Person of the Lord Jesus Christ.

The Bible may well be described as an inspired Album of divine snapshots of the Son of God. All the other characters in the group pictures fade into the background as He who is the central figure of the Bible becomes more and more clear.

Progressive Revelation

The Bible is a progressive revelation of one central Person — the Lord Jesus. A famous preacher many years ago called the Bible the "Unfolding Drama of Redemption," beginning in the very opening verses of Genesis with the seed of the woman crushing the head of the serpent, and bursting into full glory in the last book of the Bible — the *Revelation* of Jesus Christ. At first we see Him but faintly in the distance, but as the Bible is built, book by book, it becomes more and more clear as each picture of Him gives a more detailed portrait of Him. As the Bible gives more and more close-ups of Him, we recognize more and more of the details of His wonderful redemption. These close-ups of the one Person, Jesus, are given to us by many spiritual photographers and artists, covering many hundreds of years, but there is nevertheless perfect unity and purpose among them all. They begin by giving faint outlines, and each new author as he arrives on the scene adds some more details, until at last we have the composite picture of the Eternal Son of God, Son of Man, Redeemer and Saviour of the world.

WORD PICTURES

In speaking of the Bible as a picture Book we mean, of course, (as we have pointed out before) that it contains *word* pictures, verbal descriptions of the central Person of the Book. The Bible is not illustrated by pen sketches, cartoons, or pictorial figures of Christ. The Bible instead abounds in *word* pictures, conveying to our mind by the use of words the revelation of the Lord Jesus. These *word* pictures may be received by the eye while reading or by the ear in hearing. Paul tells us that

> . . . faith cometh by hearing, and hearing by the word of God (Romans 10:17).

God's ordained method of revealing His Son is by the preaching of the Word, through the hearing of the ear. Literature that is giving the message through the eye is valuable in preparing people to *hear* the Word, and exceedingly useful in instructing believers after they have *heard* the Word, but it cannot take the place of *preaching* in bringing salvation. Our commission is still,

... Go ye into all the world, and *preach the gospel* ...
(Mark 16:15).

Yes, faith still cometh by hearing and hearing by the Word
of God. Jesus Christ is the Word of God, and it is by hearing about Him, the Word of God, that men and women
must be saved. But the Bible is also called the Word of God,
and of this it is also true that faith comes by hearing the
Word. The Bible as the Word of God is the only source of
information which we have of Jesus, the Living Word of God.
The reverse is also true. No one can understand the written
Word of God, the Bible, without knowing the *Living, Incarnate Word* of God, Jesus Christ. The two are inseparable.
Destroy one and you destroy both. We repeat, therefore:
one cannot know the incarnate, living *Word* of God, Jesus
Christ, apart from the written Word, the Bible, for it is our
only source of information. But it is equally true that one
cannot know the written Word, the Bible, without knowing
Him who is the eternal Living Word incarnate, Jesus Christ.

ATTACK UPON THE BIBLE

This will explain the repeated and vicious attempts of the
enemy to disprove the historicity and authenticity of the
Bible, for in so doing one also destroys the authority of
Jesus Christ. When Jesus was on earth there was no New
Testament written. The only Scriptures that men had were
the thirty-nine books of the Old Testament, and these are
called "the scriptures" in the New Testament. These Old
Testament writings have been repeatedly called in question
and brutally attacked by the skeptics and unbelievers. Lead-
ing magazines, school books, newspapers, and other literary
works boldly assert that we can no more accept the Old
Testament literally in this age of scientific progress. They
tell us that the Bible is full of mistakes and errors, the first
five books of the Bible were not written by Moses at all, and
the early chapters of Genesis are pure mythology and fairy
tales, much like Aesop's fables, with a moral lesson but with-

out historical fact. But if there are errors in the Bible, among many historical truths, then who is going to be the infallible judge who can tell us which is fact and which is fable? It is either *all* or *nothing!* Either the Bible is the infallible Word of God, or it is not. And if you can point out one error in the record, then we cannot trust any of it, since we do not know how many other errors it may contain.

However, as we pointed out in the first chapter, this attack upon the written Word is in reality an attack upon Jesus Christ, the *Living Word*. As in the Garden of Eden the serpent's question was disguised as an honest quest for information, so too the critics of today would make us believe that the Bible must be subjected to the cross-examination of so-called science in a search for its real meaning and value. But it is again only a clever ruse to destroy the Person of the Book. We therefore again assert that the fact that Jesus accepted the Scriptures, and especially the Book of Genesis, as a true historic, authentic record settles not only the veracity of the Bible, but also the infallibility of Jesus Christ. So we ask once more, What did Jesus think of the books of Moses? Did He accept them as a literal account of creation and the beginnings of the human race? His answer is emphatically in the positive. In spite of the pious insinuations of neo-orthodoxy, Jesus leaves no doubt about His estimate of the historic, literal account of the Book of Genesis. We might refer you to numerous instances of our Lord's endorsement of the first book of Moses, but we mention just two because these have been the point of so much critical attack. They are the Flood and the story of the destruction of Sodom and Gomorrah. The skeptics who will not accept the miraculous and the supernatural discredit the story of the great Flood and the building of the Ark of Noah. But what did Jesus think about all this? He leaves no doubt about the matter at all. In Luke 17 our Lord, in speaking of the last days, says:

> And as it was in the days of Noe, so shall it be also in the days of the Son of man.
>
> They did eat, they drank, they married wives, they were given in marriage, until the day that Noe entered into the ark, and the flood came, and destroyed them all (Luke 17:26, 27).

Evidently Jesus accepted the record of the Flood as a literal historical fact. Was Jesus completely mistaken? Those who deny the story of Noah and the Ark would evidently have us think so. How about the miracle of the destruction of Sodom and the record of Lot's wife turning into a pillar of salt? Listen to what Jesus thought about this. We read in Luke 17:

> Likewise also as it was in the days of Lot; they did eat, they drank, they bought, they sold, they planted, they builded:
>
> But the same day that Lot went out of Sodom it rained fire and brimstone from heaven, and destroyed them all.
>
> Even thus shall it be in the day when the Son of man is revealed.
>
> Remember Lot's wife (Luke 17:28-30, 32).

Need anything be added to show how Jesus considered the early chapters of Genesis? Can't you see that if we could prove the historic, literal record of the Flood and Lot's wife to be merely folklore, that it would destroy all faith in the words of the Lord Jesus Christ Himself? The attack upon the Word of God, the Bible, which is gaining such momentum in these latter days, is in reality an attack upon the living, incarnate Word of God, the eternal Son of God, and the virgin-born Son of Man.

It Is All or Nothing

The Bible, therefore, is all the infallible revelation of Jesus Christ, or it is a worthless piece of silly literature for gullible fools. *It is all or nothing!* It is all true or it is false. However, the attack of Satan's emissaries does not end with a denial of the miraculous in the Bible, but it extends even to those portions which are purely historical. Many critics of the Bible assert without any substantiating facts that even father Abraham was not a historical figure. But once again Jesus has given His answer to these unbelievers when He says to the infidels of His day in John 8:58,

> . . . Before Abraham was, I am.

The word pictures of the Christ are etched upon every page of the Scriptures, if we only had the spiritual perception to recognize the outline. At first these references to Christ are vague and indefinite, and can only be recognized as we read the rest of the Scriptures, and then all becomes clear and plain. We find the first mention of Jesus in the very opening verse of the Bible. The Bible opens with the words,

> In the beginning God created the heaven and the earth (Genesis 1:1).

If we read no farther than this we would never recognize a reference to Jesus Christ in this verse. But when we go to the New Testament we read in John 1,

> In the beginning was the Word, and the Word was with God, and the Word was God.
> The same was in the beginning with God.
> All things were made by him; and without him was not any thing made that was made (John 1:1-3).

Now all is clear, for the God of creation in Genesis 1 was the same as the Word of God, Jesus Christ, or John 1. That this great Creator, the Word of God, was Jesus Christ, is established beyond a shadow of doubt by John 1:14 where the Spirit says:

> And the Word was made flesh, and dwelt among us, (and we beheld his glory, the glory as of the only begotten of the Father,) full of grace and truth.

Jesus Christ as the Word of God is the Creator of Heaven and earth, and all that happened afterward was by Him as the Word of God. No less than ten times in Genesis, chapter 1, do we read the phrase, "And God said." It was by the Word of God that all things were created. Paul says, in Colossians, concerning the Lord Jesus:

> For by him were all things created, that are in heaven, and that are in earth, visible and invisible, whether they be thrones, or dominions, or principalities, or powers: all things were created by him, and for him:
> And he is before all things, and by him all things consist (Colossians 1:16, 17).

David says in Psalm 33:

> By the word of the Lord were the heavens made . . . (Psalm 33:6).

Since Christ is the Word of creation, He is the Creator. So we see that in the very opening verse of the Bible we already are brought face to face with a picture of the Man of the Book — the Lord Jesus. To be sure, without the rest of the Bible we would not be able to identify Jesus Christ in Genesis, but the rest of the Scriptures illuminates the faint outline so there is no doubt as to who is meant when we read:

> In the beginning God created the heaven and the earth (Genesis 1:1).

In the following chapters we shall follow the progress of these Word pictures of Jesus as the light of revelation shows more and more of the details of His infinitely perfect person. Surely with the full light of the Scriptures today, there is no excuse for anyone's failing to see Him as the only Saviour and Redeemer.

3

CHRIST AND ADAM'S RIB

And beginning at Moses and all the prophets, he expounded unto them in all the scriptures the things concerning himself (Luke 24:27).

Do you remember the old family album of years ago?
That ornate, bulky book full of snapshots and photos of the
family, the uncles and aunts, together with notations of special events? In the front of the book was the family data
of births and marriages, and tear-stained records of deaths.
But the pictures were the things that intrigued us most.
Those old tintypes of father and mother in their old-fashioned
clothes, grandfather with his long beard, and then the picture of one's self as a baby with a little embroidered jacket
and the long, long dress. The pictures were a continued
story — the history of the family.

Now the Bible is such a picture Book. It is a collection
of portraits of one supreme Person who overshadows all the
rest of the pictures. The central object of this Bible Album
is Jesus Christ, the Son of God and the Son of man. He is
the central figure on every page, and the other pictures
grouped about Him are added only to bring into bolder relief the loveliness, the superlative beauty, the infinite perfection of the Man of the Book, the Lord Jesus.

On Every Page

The face of Jesus Christ is on every page of Scripture. Every single incident recorded in the Word, in some way, directly or indirectly, has some connection with God's revelation concerning Him. This our Lord Jesus Himself taught when He spoke to the two disciples on the way to Emmaus on that first resurrection day. These disciples were returning from Jerusalem, sad and depressed because their Lord had been crucified. Jesus joined them and inquired into the cause of their sadness, and then astonished them with the statement that all this had been foretold in the Bible. If they had only known the Scriptures they would not have been sad but rejoicing. Listen to His words of loving rebuke:

> . . . O fools, and slow of heart to believe *all* that the prophets have spoken:
> Ought not Christ to have suffered these things, and to enter into his glory? (Luke 24:25, 26).

And then after this rebuke for their tragic neglect to believe *all* the Scriptures, we read the amazing statement of our text:

> And beginning at Moses and all the prophets, he expounded unto them in *all* the scriptures the things concerning himself (Luke 24:27).

Jesus says that *all* the Scriptures speak of Him. Now the Scriptures to which Jesus referred were the Old Testament. Not a single line of the New Testament had as yet been written when He spoke these words. It is of the Old Testament Jesus declares that they *all* speak of Him. The Old Testament, therefore, is not primarily an account of creation, the history of the Hebrew nation, or a collection of moral, religious and ethical instructions, but it is a *revelation of Jesus Christ.*

TRANSFORMS THE BIBLE

Once we realize that the Old Testament is a revelation of the Lord Jesus, and we must find Him somewhere on every page, the study of the Old Testament will be transformed from a dull and wearying task, to a thrilling, exciting exercise as we look for *His face,* hidden among the incidents recorded in the Book. This is what Jesus meant when He said,

> Search the scriptures; . . . they are they which testify of me (John 5:39).

PICTURES OF THE CHRIST

In the succeeding chapters we shall seek to point out a few of the innumerable portraits of the Lord Jesus in the Old Testament, with the fervent prayer that it may stimulate you to find for yourself new and precious visions of His glory. Our Lord said to the disciples on the road to Emmaus that *all* the Scriptures, beginning with Moses, spoke of Him. So we turn to the first few "pages" of our picture album, the books of Moses. The reference is to the first five books of the Bible written by Moses, which are Genesis, Exodus, Leviticus, Numbers, and Deuteronomy. The picture album of the Old Testament has thirty-nine pages, and on every page we may find portraits, pen sketches, profiles, full length portraits, and candid camera shots of this Altogether Lovely One.

PAGE NUMBER ONE

Page number one in our album is the Book of Genesis. Most people associate Genesis with the record of creation and the early history of the human race. But this is only secondary. The primary purpose of Genesis is to introduce to us the Lord Jesus. Before we take up a few of these portraits, let me say that without the New Testament it would be impossible to see these wonderful revelations of Christ.

They are in miniature, and with the naked eye we can behold only the dimmest outlines. But now comes the New Testament and illumines and magnifies these portraits until all is clear. You remember the hours we spent as children looking through a stereopticon at slides of some of the wonders of the world. We called it a magic lantern because when we mounted two pictures and then looked at them through the binoculars, the two pictures blended into one, bringing out all the details in bold and clear relief. Today we, of course, have greatly improved upon this by small colored slides and a projector which greatly magnifies the otherwise dim and undistinguishable outlines and throws them clearly on the screen.

Such is the relationship of the Old and the New Testament. The Old Testament is an album of slides, painted by the Holy Spirit, but they can only be fully understood and appreciated as we view them in the light of the New Testament which is the magic lantern through which we see the infinite beauties of the Lord Jesus in the Old.

MANY PICTURES

In the previous chapter we pointed out that the very first sentence in the Bible is a picture of Jesus Christ. It will bear repeating. The opening verse is:

> In the beginning God created the heaven and the earth (Genesis 1:1).

This is a picture of the Lord Jesus, but we could never recognize it as such until we look at it through the magic lantern of the New Testament. And when we do that, we see Him, for John says:

> In the beginning was the Word, and the Word was with God, and the Word was God.
> The same was in the beginning with God.
> All things were made by him; and without him was not any thing made that was made (John 1:1-3).

The picture is clear. The first portrait on page one of God's Album is a picture of Christ the Creator of all things. And now we can go on to the next photo. It is a picture of darkness and gloom, destruction and chaos. It is an earth without form and void, upon which the Spirit of God began to move in preparation for the next act in creation.

> And God said, Let there be light: and there was light (Genesis 1:3).

That is the picture, and as we set it in the frame and look at it in the light of God's full revelation, we see Jesus. He is the Light of the world. John says:

> In him [Jesus] was life; and the life was the light of men (John 1:4).

And Jesus Himself declares, at the healing of the blind man,

> . . . I am the light of the world (John 9:5).

> . . . I am the light of the world: he that followeth me shall not walk in darkness, but shall have the light of life (John 8:12).

> I am come a light into the world, that whosoever believeth on me should not abide in darkness (John 12:46).

The rest of the record of the seven days of creation is but an expansion of the work of the Lord Jesus. The second day of creation, God separated the waters on earth from those in the heavens. Jesus, the Light of the World, is the Great Separator between the things of earth and the things of heaven. The presence of light attracts and awakens some, but repels and drives away others. At sunrise the birds and animals of the day awaken with song, but the same sunlight causes the unclean owls and bats and bloodthirsty beasts to seek cover under darkness. And so in the separation of the waters as the result of the light we see a picture of the work of Jesus Christ. John says:

> And this is the condemnation, that light is come into the world, and men loved darkness rather than light, because their deeds were evil.
>
> For every one that doeth evil hateth the light, neither cometh to the light, lest his deeds should be reproved.
>
> But he that doeth truth cometh to the light, that his deeds may be made manifest, that they are wrought in God (John 3:19-21).

We can find Christ in every other day of creation, until it consummates in the creation of man in the image of God. Adam is a picture of Christ and He is called in the Bible the "second man" (I Corinthians 15:47), and the "last Adam" (I Corinthians 15:45). Many men in the Scriptures are types of the Lord Jesus, such as Abel, Isaac, Jacob, Joseph, David, and many others, but very few ever think of Adam as a type and portrait of the Lord Jesus. We shall have occasion to point this out in detail in a later chapter, but right here let me call your attention to one superlatively beautiful picture. It is the creation of Eve as the wife of Adam. God "caused a deep sleep to fall upon Adam, and he slept: and he [God] took one of his ribs, and closed up the flesh instead thereof" (Genesis 2:21).

While Adam slept, God created from his wounded side, a wife, who was part of himself, and he paid for her by the shedding of blood. And after Adam awoke he said:

> . . . This is now bone of my bones, and flesh of my flesh: she shall be called Woman, because she was taken out of Man.
>
> Therefore shall a man leave his father and his mother, and shall cleave unto his wife: and they shall be one flesh (Genesis 2:23, 24).

THE DIM PICTURE

There is the slide, but we will never know its meaning until we behold it through the binoculars of the New Testament. Then we stand breathless with wonder, awe, and adoration at its beauty, and prostrate ourselves in adoration before *Him*, the *last Adam*, the *Man of the glory*. Let the Apostle Paul turn on the magic lantern for us. He snaps it on in Ephesians 5, among many other places. Speaking of the union of believers in Christ he says:

> For we are members of his body, of his flesh, and of his bones (Ephesians 5:30).

This is a direct reference to the words of Adam when he said, "she is bone of my bone and flesh of my flesh."
And then Paul quotes from Genesis, and says:

> For this cause shall a man leave his father and mother, and shall be joined unto his wife, and they two shall be one flesh.
> This is a great mystery: but I speak concerning Christ and the church (Ephesians 5:31, 32).

Now all is clear. Adam is a picture of the Lord Jesus, who left His Father's house to gain His bride at the price of His own life. Jesus, the last Adam, like the first, must be put to sleep to purchase His Bride, the Church, and Jesus died on the cross and slept in the tomb for three days and three nights. His side too was opened after He had fallen asleep, and from that wounded side redemption flowed. I believe that in the creation of Eve, Adam gave his literal blood. God opened his side and this implies a wound and blood-shedding. Here then at the very dawn of creation, even before man had fallen, we have an implied reference to a new creature taken from the side of a man and becoming a part of him, even of his flesh, and of his bones.

FULFILLED IN CHRIST

The Church, which is His body, was also purchased by the Lord Jesus Christ. It meant His death, asleep for three days and three nights. His side too was opened, and the cleansing water and His justifying blood flowed forth. The Church, like Eve, was a new creation, not by a natural birth, but by a supernatural operation of God, and this "rib" was builded into a woman who was to become the helpmeet and bride of the husband. How long a time elapsed between the "operation" on Adam's side, and the completion of the task of building the rib into a wife we are not told, but it is implied that there was a period of time between the removal of the rib, and the completion of Eve and her presentation to Adam. There are two steps clearly indicated:

1. The operation — God "took one of his ribs and closed up the flesh instead thereof."
2. God brought her unto the man.

Between these two steps is the record, "And the rib which the Lord God had taken from man made he a woman." And when the building of the woman was complete He brought the man and the "rib" back together. The word translated "made" in our Scripture in the original is *bannah,* and occurs scores of times in the rest of the Bible, but only in this passage and in Ezekiel 27:5 is it translated "made." In all the other places it is translated "build." So the verse should read, "And the rib which the Lord God had taken from man *builded* he into a woman." How long it took to build the woman we do not know, but God separated the man from the rib until the building was done and then He "brought her unto the man."

This is the picture of our great Redeemer as seen on page one of God's picture Album. Jesus died on the cross, His side was opened, and by the Holy Spirit today a Bride is being prepared, and when the last member has been added He will bring her unto the man Christ Jesus. God has been "building" this precious Bride, purchased by His blood, for the past nineteen hundred years, and soon she will be presented to her Lord. That will be the consummation. Paul says that,

> . . . Christ also loved the church, and gave himself for it;
> That he might sanctify and cleanse it with the washing of water by the word,

That he might present it to himself a glorious church, not having spot, or wrinkle, or any such thing; but that it should be holy and without blemish (Ephesians 5: 25-27).

This is a great mystery: but I speak concerning Christ and the church (Ephesians 5:32).

4

CHRIST THE SECOND MAN

Many years ago in the city of Detroit, Michigan, a prominent businessman wandered into our Friday Night Bible Class purely out of curiosity about the large crowd assembled there. But before the meeting ended, the Holy Spirit had done His work, and the man remained after the meeting to talk with me, and was genuinely converted and saved by the Holy Spirit's application of the Word of God to his heart. We became fast friends, and one day he presented me with a 16 millimeter movie camera, together with a projector, editor, and other accessories for taking movies. It was the beginning of my interest in taking pictures, and for a few years I took quite a number of reels of scenes, many of them pictures of the family. Then after a while the activity seemed to wane, and for the past couple of years I have taken scarcely any pictures at all. Just recently my grandson developed an interest in the pictures which had been carefully preserved for over a period of more than twenty years. We began by showing pictures of the family when the children were still small, and then successive scenes pictured them a little older, and then later some when they were mature. Then came the grandchildren and we watched them grow up on film. It was all intensely interesting to see the growth of these loved ones from infancy to full manhood.

Bible a Library of Pictures

Looking at these pictures reminded me of the Bible as a library of progressive pictures of one central Person, the Lord Jesus Christ. From Genesis to Revelation we have a series of portraits of the Son of God. The first pictures are often faint and can only be recognized by the later ones which increase in clarity and detail as the light of inspiration illumines the types and shadows and outlines of His Person. In our previous chapter we saw the outline of Jesus in the opening verse of the Bible:

> In the beginning God created the heaven and the earth (Genesis 1:1).

In the light of the New Testament we know that this great Creator was none other than the Lord Jesus. God the Father, through His Son, the Word of God, created all things for His glory. Then we saw that Adam was a picture of the Lord Jesus who was the Second Man and the last Adam. While Adam slept, God was building a bride for him from a rib taken from his side. We know this is a picture of the Lord Jesus, for Paul informs us in Ephesians 5 that as Eve was a member of the body of Adam, so are we as believers members of His body. He says:

> For we are members of his body, of his flesh, and of his bones (Ephesians 5:30).

The Protevangelium

In the third chapter of Genesis we meet another unmistakable portrait of the coming Redeemer in our Album of word pictures of Christ. It is the verse usually spoken of theologically as the *protevangelium*, which simply indicates that it is the first mention of a coming Redeemer, after the first man Adam had sinned and become estranged from His creator. God had given him the complete and full enjoyment of the Garden of Eden with just one exception, "the tree of the knowledge of good and evil." The Lord had plainly made His will known to Adam when He said:

> And the Lord God commanded the man, saying, Of every tree of the garden thou mayest freely eat:
> But of the tree of the knowledge of good and evil, thou shalt not eat of it: for in the day that thou eatest thereof thou shalt surely die (Genesis 2:16, 17).

God spoke these words to Adam *before* Eve was created. Therefore, Eve did not hear what God said to her husband. She only knew it by hearsay, which may account for the fact that Satan did not tempt Adam directly, but accomplished it through his wife, Eve. And right here we have a picture of Christ and His love for His fallen Bride. Adam is not usually thought of as a *type of Christ*. He is usually contrasted with Christ, but the Bible teaches that Adam was a clear, unmistakable picture of Christ as the Saviour and Redeemer of the Church, His chosen Bride. Please follow very carefully the revelation of this mystery as revealed in the New Testament. Paul, in speaking about the relationship of husband and wife, says,

> For this cause shall a man leave his father and mother, and shall be joined unto his wife, and they two shall be one flesh (Ephesians 5:31).

This is a direct, almost word for word quotation from Genesis 2:24 where we read:

> Therefore shall a man leave his father and his mother, and shall cleave unto his wife: and they shall be one flesh (Genesis 2:24).

THE GREAT MYSTERY

The next verse (Ephesians 5:32) is the important one, so do not miss it. If you miss the point of this verse, you will be unable to understand that which follows. Here is the verse:

> This is a great mystery: but I speak concerning Christ
> and the church (Ephesians 5:32).

What is this great mystery? Is it the fact that a man shall leave his father and mother and cleave to his wife, even at the cost of death? That is no mystery. It is the most natural thing in all the earth. The mystery Paul speaks of is that Jesus Christ, the spotless Son of God, should be willing to leave His Father's house and come into the world to save a filthy, fallen, unfaithful "wife," even by dying on the cross for her. This is the mystery, and Paul calls it a *great mystery,* and adds, "but I speak concerning Christ and the church." Adam therefore becomes a type of Christ in His relation to His beloved Bride. Remember then that according to Paul, Adam is a type, a picture of Christ in His love for His Bride, the Church.

LOVE CAUSED ADAM'S SIN

Adam's love for Eve is a faint but unmistakable picture of the love of our Lord Jesus for His chosen own. Soon after God had said to Adam, "for this cause shall a man cleave unto his wife," the tempter came to *Eve* and not to Adam. Adam was the head of Eve, and if the tempter had caused Adam to sin it would naturally include Eve. However, Adam was not directly tempted, but instead, by way of his wife. When Eve fell she fell as an individual — not as the federal head. Logically the quickest way for Satan to cause man's ruin would be by a direct attack upon Adam, but instead he chose to tempt Adam *through his wife,* Eve. There must be a reason and the reason is not hard to find in view of Paul's words in Ephesians 5. Satan probably knew he could not sway Adam, for God's words were fresh in his ears. But Eve never heard God's word about the forbidden tree. She had only received it "second-hand" through Adam, for remember, Eve was not yet created when God gave the prohibition. This may be one reason why Satan came to the woman instead of the man.

The real reason, however, went deeper. Satan must have known the intense love of Adam for Eve (a love that was far stronger and purer than any since then between husband and wife). Satan hoped to make this love of Adam for his wife the cause for him to fall to her level. But still another fact must have entered in. Adam knew God in a perfect way as no human since has known. He knew God was a holy God. He knew what the penalty of sin was, for he understood when God said, "in the day that thou eatest thereof thou shalt surely die" (Genesis 2:17).

Now his wife whom he loved more than himself had transgressed God's command and *must die*. But in addition to this, he had lost his bride, for Adam was still innocent and holy before God, while Eve was a fallen sinner under sentence of death. Communion between them had been broken. An infinite gulf now separated them. They were no longer one. Eve was a lost sinner; Adam still a son of God (Luke 3:38). But Adam loved Eve above all things, and immediately cast about for a way to save her and make her again his own. But Adam also must have known that for Eve to be redeemed, it must be by a human redeemer, later referred to as the *seed of the woman*. Eve needed a Redeemer, a Saviour, and this Saviour must be *her seed*. None else but a human can atone for human sin. But how could Eve bring forth a *seed* without a husband? Adam could not be the father of her seed as long as he was separated from her by her sin. She was the only woman, Adam the only man, and they were separated by the infinite gulf of sin. In Adam's perfect state he could have no communion with fallen Eve (II Corinthians 6:14-16).

How could this gulf be bridged? How could communion be restored? Eve could not be raised to Adam's level of innocence without a redeemer, and that Redeemer must be the seed of the woman, and the only man who could become the father of that seed was Adam. Since Adam could not lift

Eve to his level without the Redeemer seed, he must lower himself to her level, assume her guilt, become partaker of her sin and condemnation, and then, the separation between them being removed, he could become the father of her seed. And so Adam deliberately, willingly, and with full knowledge of the consequence, took the fruit from Eve's hand and "did eat." He had stooped to her level in order to save her by becoming the only one who could bring forth the *seed of the woman — the Redeemer.*

Adam Was Not Deceived

Adam had now made Eve's sin his own responsibility, and makes himself subject to *death* by becoming partaker of the curse of death upon Eve. Perchance some of you have raised your eyebrows at this interpretation, and are planning to register your objections. Before you do, let me point you to some other Scripture passages which fully confirm this interpretation. Paul in writing to Timothy emphasizes the subordinate place of the wife to her husband, and gives as his reason the fact that Eve, the first wife, owed her salvation to her husband (I Timothy 2:12, 13). And then Paul gives the reason:

> And Adam was not deceived, but the woman being deceived was in the transgression (I Timothy 2:14).

Notice those words — *Adam was not deceived.* He knew what he was doing. He knew the full consequences of his act. He knew it meant his death, but it was the only way to save his beloved bride. And this salvation would be by the bearing of a child. Eve must become a mother of a baby, the seed, to be saved. Adam was the only one who could bring this about. And so Paul continues:

> Notwithstanding she shall be saved in childbearing, if they continue in faith and charity and holiness with sobriety (I Timothy 2:15).

Literally this verse means, "Although the woman was deceived, she shall be saved by the *bearing of a child*." The original text makes this clear. In the original it is *dia tes teknogonias* — "*through the bearing of a child*." Eve must have a seed, and only Adam's love for her made this possible, but it meant his death.

TYPE OF CHRIST

In all of this, Adam was a type of Christ. This is established beyond possible contradiction for:

> Nevertheless death reigned from Adam to Moses, even over them that had not sinned after the similitude of Adam's transgression, *who is the figure of him that was to come* (Romans 5:14).

Adam's transgression was different from any other. We sin because we are sinners. Adam became a sinner because he deliberately chose to share in the sin of Eve. In this he was the *figure* (*a type*) of Jesus Christ. Now of course the type can never do justice to the antitype.

Jesus also loved the Church, His Bride, and gave Himself for it. His Bride too had been deceived by the enemy and alienated from God. But see the great love which Jesus had for His fallen Bride: He left His Father's house and came down to the level of fallen man, made man's sin His responsibility, and stooped even unto death, to save His beloved. When Adam stooped to save Eve, he became a sinner. This, of course, was not true of Jesus, for He knew no sin. Yet He identified Himself with our sin, and did even more than Adam, for II Corinthians 5:21 says,

> For he hath made him to be sin for us, who knew no sin; that we might be made the righteousness of God in him.

Jesus took our sin upon Himself. It meant His death, but His love knew no bounds. He bore our sins in His own body on the tree. This is the great mystery Paul refers to when he says:

> For this cause shall a man leave his father and mother, and shall be joined unto his wife, and they two shall be one flesh.
> *This is a great mystery*: but I speak concerning *Christ and the church* (Ephesians 5:31, 32).

Oh, how He loved us!

5

CHRIST THE WILLING SERVANT

The revelation of the Bible is centered around one Person — the Lord Jesus Christ, the Son of God. He Himself said, "Search the scriptures; . . . they are they which testify of me" (John 5:39). In studying the Bible a person has never reached the real heart of any passage until he has seen in it the outline of the face of the Redeemer. In the story of creation, the record of the Flood, the history of the patriarchs, even in the records of the wars of Israel, we can find the outline of His person, we can trace His footprints, if we only look closely enough. In our previous chapters we found Him in the very first verse of Genesis 1, as the One who as the Word of God created all things.

Then we briefly studied the record of Adam, the first man, and discovered in that story a picture of Calvary, as God put Adam to sleep (symbolizing death), opened his side and took out a bloody rib, and builded it into a woman to be the bride of the first man. This we saw was an unmistakable picture of the Second Man, Jesus, the last Adam, who took our sin and its penalty, death, so that from His wounded side the Church might be born. In our last chapter we saw Adam as a picture of Christ in his love for Eve after she had fallen into sin. A great gulf now separated Adam from his wife, for she was a sinner estranged from God, while Adam was still perfect as he came from the hand of God. With this gulf between them there could be no communion or contact. But Adam loved his wife with an all-consuming love. Adam knew that unless something were done to bridge this gulf, he had lost Eve forever. Adam also knew that the only way Eve could be redeemed was by a kinsman redeemer — her own seed. The Redeemer must be a human being, a member of the human race. In other words it must be the seed of the woman. Eve was the only person who could bring forth this seed, for she was the only woman in existence. However to bring forth this seed, she must have a husband, and there was only one man in existence who could be her husband and he (Adam) was completely separated from her by her sin. In order for Eve to bring forth the Redeemer seed it was necessary for the gulf between Adam and his wife to be bridged. Since Adam could not lift her to his holy level without the Redeemer, there was only one other way. He must stoop to where she lay. And this Adam did when he took the forbidden fruit from Eve's hand and became a sinner with her. This Adam did voluntarily with his eyes wide open, and with full knowledge of its consequences, death for himself. But his love drove him to assume Eve's guilt and bear her penalty in order to save her.

The Bible is crystal-clear on this great mystery, for after Paul says concerning Adam, "For this cause shall a man leave his father and mother, and shall be joined unto his wife . . ." (Ephesians 5:31), he adds, "This is a great mystery: but I speak concerning Christ and the church" (Ephesians 5:32). All doubt as to the meaning of these words is dispelled by Paul's statement in I Timothy 2:14 where he declares, "And Adam was not deceived but the woman being deceived was in the transgression." And Paul tells us in Romans 5:14 that in all this Adam was a "figure (type) of him that was to come."

Jesus Our Redeemer

We too had been deceived by Satan and were lost, under sentence of eternal death and Hell. But Jesus saw our plight

and willingly left His Father's house to come *down* to where
we lay in death, assume our debt, and by death and resurrection redeem us. This made necessary the *Incarnation* of the
Son of God, for remember, the Redeemer must be the *seed
of the woman.* He must be the offspring of fallen Eve. This
necessitated the Virgin Birth. But this raises an important
question. From beginningless eternity until His Incarnation
nineteen hundred years ago, *Jesus was not a man!* He was a
Spirit, one of the three persons of the Trinity. Although at
times He temporarily assumed a human *form*, called a Chris-
tophany, He did not permanently take on a human body and
human nature until He was born as a babe in Bethlehem.
So we repeat, from a beginningless eternity until less than
two thousand years ago Jesus had no human body. He was
not the seed of the woman. To redeem us, therefore, He came
as the promised seed, took on a human form in which He went
to the cross, arose from the tomb, ascended into Heaven, and
will come again as the divine, human Jesus to set up His
Kingdom.

And Then After That!

If Jesus became incarnate in a human body only to save us,
then the question arises, "Will He then surrender His humanity when His work of redemption is fully complete?" I
want you to get this question clearly. If Jesus took on His
humanity to save us, then does it not seem reasonable that He
should again lay aside this humanity, once the work of redemption is full and complete? Will He then go back into
that invisible Spirit being which He had before His Incarnation? I say, He would have a legal, reasonable right to do so,
but *will He?* The Bible gives the answer. After time has run
its course, and God's program is complete and time gives way
to eternity, Christ will still forever remain human. After the
millennium is over, the earth has been purified by fire, the
last redeemed one is safe in Heaven, and all the lost forever
in Hell, then will Jesus exercise His legal prerogative to lay

aside the form of man which He assumed only to redeem us, and go back into the invisible form of God He had from eternity? Listen to the answer of Scripture:

> And when all things shall be subdued unto him, then shall the Son also himself be subject unto him that put all things under him, that God may be all in all (I Corinthians 15:28).

When the last enemy, death, has been destroyed (I Corinthians 15:25, 26) and eternal bliss ushered in, Jesus (though He has a legal right to lay aside the Incarnation — the badge of redemption) will choose to remain a *Man* that He may be forever with His own as *one of them.* The verse we quoted, "then shall the Son be subject," should read "then shall the Son *remain* subject unto him that hath put all things under him." All this is in harmony with the words of Paul in Ephesians:

> For this cause shall a man . . . be joined unto his wife, and they two shall be one flesh.
> This is a great mystery: but I speak concerning Christ and the church (Ephesians 5:31, 32).

It will be the ultimate fulfillment of the promise, "I will never leave thee, nor forsake thee" (Hebrews 13:5).

This then is a picture of Jesus Christ way back in Genesis 3. It is most clearly illustrated by another picture of this same thing in the next book of the Bible — Exodus. Among the many civil laws of Israel was one law providing for the redemption of slaves. We call your attention to Exodus 21:2-6,

> If thou buy an Hebrew servant, six years he shall serve: and in the seventh he shall go free for nothing.
> If he came in by himself [single], he shall go out by himself [single]: if he were married, then his wife shall go out with him.
> [But] If his master have given him a wife, and she have born him sons or daughters; the wife and her children shall be her master's, and he shall [can] go out by himself.

> And [but] if the servant shall plainly say, I love my
> master, my wife, and my children; I will not go out
> free:
>
> Then his master shall bring him unto the judges; he
> shall also bring him to the door, or unto the door post;
> and his master shall bore his ear through with an aul;
> and he shall serve him for ever.

This was a law in Israel. If a person sold himself in servitude to another in payment of a debt, he could not be made to
serve more than six years. After that the debt was considered
paid, and the man could go out free. However, if during the
six years of service his master had given him a wife, the wife
was to remain in the service of the master and only the man
was permitted to go free. If the husband refused to leave his
wife behind because of his love for her, he was required to
remain a servant the rest of his life as the price for remain-
ing with his wife. If a man declared that he refused his
liberty after six years because of his love for his wife, an impressive ceremony was required. The slave was taken to the
gate of the city before the judges, where he declared his in-
tention of surrendering his liberty for love of his wife. The
judges then would take a sharp aul, and pierce his ear, leaving a permanent scar, as a symbol of his unending subjection
to his master in order that he might not be separated from his
wife. The scar resulting from the wound made by the aul
was permanent. It was in a prominent place where all could
see it, and by it be reminded that for love of his bride he had
foregone his legal liberty and voluntarily chosen to remain
in the house of servitude forever.

The Perfect Hebrew Servant

It was a badge of honor, a testimony of undying love. Now,
of course, we have no difficulty seeing in all this a picture of
the Lord Jesus Christ. He is the perfect Hebrew servant. To
pay our debt which we could not pay, He left Heaven's glory
and laid aside the form of God. He made Himself a slave

to pay our debt and subjected Himself to the Father to atone for our sin. Paul expresses this great transaction in that glorious passage concerning His servitude and humbling for our sake, in Philippians 2,

> Who, being in the form of God, thought it not robbery to be equal with God:
>
> But made himself of no reputation, and took upon him the *form of a servant* [bondslave], and was made in the likeness of men [his incarnation]:
>
> And being found in fashion as a man [his human nature and body], he humbled himself, and became obedient unto death, even the death of the cross (Philippians 2:6-8).

Christ was not always human. He has been so only for less than two thousand years. His Incarnation is the badge of His love for us. He made Himself a servant, and to redeem us went to the cross to die for us, and bears in His hands and feet the scars of the nails with which His body was pierced. The faithful servant in the Old Testament (Exodus 21) bore the scars signifying his love for his bride, in his ears. Jesus bears the scars of His love in His hands and feet and brow and back.

But God's great sabbatical year is coming. After time has run its course and eternity is ushered in, then Jesus will have a legal right to lay aside the body of flesh and bone, and go back into the form of the invisible God. I say, *He has a legal right to do so,* just as the servant in Exodus 21 had a legal right to go free, but would have to leave his wife. So too, since the body of Jesus' Incarnation was assumed solely for our redemption, He would have a perfect right to lay aside His human form and go back into the invisible form of God. Do you realize what this would mean? Suppose at the end of time Jesus should lay aside His humanity and choose to free Himself from His human ties with us, what would it mean to us? It would mean that He would be forever removed and separated from us as far as *human* relationship would be concerned. But Paul assures us He will always remain in His human form, so that we can see Him, touch Him, fellowship with Him and worship Him, as our incarnate, divine, but also human Saviour. Yes, throughout eternity we shall be with Him in His visible, tangible, precious body forever and ever. In this body He will bear the marks of His loyalty and love, the scars in His hands and feet, just as the servant in the Old Testament bore the indelible scars of the wounds in his ears for everyone to see. Yes, indeed, we shall know Him by the print of the nails in His hands.

A CLOSING SCENE

In closing let us go back to the servant type in Exodus 21, to the man who surrendered his liberty and privilege of going free because of his love for his wife. Imagine with me the sunset years of this happy couple. The family has grown up, and in the evening John returns from the field to their love-filled home in the valley. We shall call the servant, John, and the wife, Mary. The sun has just sunk behind the hills and the long shadows are darkening the room where Mary sits looking for the return of John. She has placed his favorite chair before the fireplace with its cheery, flickering flame. As John returns and settles down in his chair, Mary quietly slips up behind him, and gently strokes his forehead, and runs her fingers lovingly through his graying hair. Her hands slip over his ears, and her fingers once more fondle the precious scars made by the aul so many years ago. The tears begin to fall, for she recalls the meaning of those scars, and she whispers in his pierced ear, "Oh, John, I love you more than I ever thought I could." And then she stoops to plant a ——— , but wait, some scenes are too holy, too sacred for others to behold, so we turn away, and leave the loving couple dreaming in the gloaming of the happy days gone by.

WHAT WILL HEAVEN BE?

I don't know much about what Heaven will be, but it is enough to know that we shall be with Him. I am sure that again and again and again we shall go to Him, and in His tender embrace whisper, "Saviour, Lord and Master, let me see again your hands and your feet." I am sure the wounds He showed His disciples, and said, "Behold my hands and my feet" (Luke 24:39), will be the eternal source of our adoration and everlasting gratitude. Then we shall be able to sing as we ought, "My Jesus, I love Thee, I know Thou art mine," and the last verse of that song will become an experience of reality:

> In mansions of glory and endless delight,
> I'll ever adore Thee in heaven so bright;
> I'll sing with the glittering crown on my brow,
> If ever I loved Thee, my Jesus, 'tis now.

6

THE EVIDENCE OF THE RESURRECTION *

And I will put enmity between thee and the woman,
and between thy seed and her seed; it shall bruise thy
head, and thou shalt bruise his heel (Genesis 3:15).

If we had perfect spiritual eyesight we would be able to
trace the outline of the face of Christ on every page of the
Bible. At first the outline is dim and faint, but as we move
along in God's Album of pictures of His Son in the Bible, His
features become more clear and distinct. The Bible is first
of all and primarily a Revelation of Jesus Christ from Genesis
1:1 to Revelation 22:21. Our Lord Himself claimed this on
various occasions. We repeat once more His words on the
road to Emmaus on the day of His Resurrection. As He
walked with the two discouraged disciples and heard the
story of their disappointment, He made one of His most remarkable claims about Himself. These disciples had believed
that Jesus was the Jewish Messiah, and they so expressed it:

But we trusted that it had been he which should have
redeemed Israel: and beside all this, to day is the third
day since these things were done (Luke 24:21).

Their astonishment was greatly augmented by certain re-
ports by certain women who had been told by angels that Je-

* This chapter contains much of the actual material used on Dr. DeHaan's
final broadcast. The message was recorded on the day he died.

sus was alive again (Luke 24:23). Now they were really confused and Jesus severely rebuked them for their unbelief and failure to believe the Scriptures. Hear again His rebuke:

> Then he said unto them, O fools, and slow of heart to believe *all* that the prophets have spoken (Luke 24:25).

We call your attention to the one word, *all*. These disciples had believed the prophets but they had not believed it *all*. They chose to believe that which they liked, and rejected or disbelieved that which was unpleasant and contrary to their wishes. They had believed the prophets when they spoke of the Messiah coming in power and great glory to put down Israel's enemies and set up the Davidic Kingdom. This they were ready to believe, but when the prophets told of the Messiah being rejected by His people and put to death, this they refused to accept, so that Isaiah could cry out prophetically in Isaiah 53:

> Who hath believed our report? and to whom is the arm of the LORD revealed? (Isaiah 53:1).

Jesus rebuked these disciples for believing only part of the Word and ignoring the rest, and so He continues in Luke 24:26,

> Ought not Christ to have suffered these things, and to enter into his glory?

Why did you accept only that which pleased your thinking, and so completely ignore the part about the suffering and rejection of the Messiah? Then Jesus utters words of such tremendous weight and importance that I wish I knew how to pound them into your heads and hearts. May the Holy Spirit accent them and give you understanding of this tremendous statement by Jesus. Here it is, and pay close attention:

> And beginning at Moses and all the prophets, he expounded unto them *in all the scriptures* the things concerning himself (Luke 24:27).

Notice in this verse two statements:

1. Beginning at Moses.
2. In all the Scriptures.

BEGINNING AT MOSES

As Jesus expounded to them the things which Moses and all the prophets had said about Him, they were not aware of the fact He was speaking of Himself. They didn't know it was this very Jesus who was talking to them. Who He was they did not know, but this Man was telling them things about Jesus they never knew before. No wonder they constrained Him to come into their house. They wanted this strange Man to tell them more about Jesus in the books of Moses and in all the Scriptures. Later, while they were listening and eating up His words, this Man took bread and He broke it, after blessing it, and handed it to them. Suddenly they "woke up" and recognized that it was Jesus Himself who had been expounding the Scriptures to them.

HOW DID THEY RECOGNIZE HIM?

I often wondered how these two disciples recognized it was Jesus Himself. I know the Scripture says that "their eyes were opened, and they knew him" (Luke 24:31). But what did they see when their eyes were opened? I think we have the answer in their report to the rest of the disciples. After they had recognized Jesus they immediately returned to Jerusalem to report to the eleven and a company of others.

> And they told what things were done in the way, and how he was known of them in breaking of bread (Luke 24:35).

Notice two things: (1) they told about Jesus' *opening* of the Scriptures from Moses on; and (2) how they recognized Him. It was in the breaking of the bread. Notice the words:

> . . . and how he was known of them in breaking of bread (Luke 24:35).

As Jesus took the bread and broke it and handed it to them, they saw His identification marks — *the wounds in His hands.* As He passed the bread to them they beheld His hands. The wounded hands of Jesus were His identification. Later on we have the same story. While these two disciples were telling of meeting Jesus in the way, suddenly Jesus Himself appears in their midst:

> But they were terrified and affrighted, and supposed that they had seen a spirit.
>
> And he said unto them, Why are ye troubled? and why do thoughts arise in your hearts?
>
> *Behold my hands and my feet,* that it is I myself: . . .
>
> And when he had thus spoken, he shewed them his hands and his feet (Luke 24:37-40).

The same story is repeated in the experience of Thomas. Thomas had said he would not believe until he saw the evidence. One week later Jesus appears to the disciples and singling out Thomas, He says:

> . . . Reach hither thy finger, and behold my hands; and reach hither thy hand, and thrust it into my side: and be not faithless, but believing (John 20:27).

WHAT WAS WRONG?

What was wrong with these disciples of Jesus that they were so slow to recognize Him and believe Him? It was because they had not believed *all* the Scriptures concerning Christ. They had accepted only that which met with their wishful thinking, and the rest they ignored. They were glad to believe that when Messiah came He would deliver Israel, restore the Davidic Kingdom, and bring in the age of peace and righteousness. That was all quite acceptable to them, but those parts of the Scriptures which told of His suffering and rejection they either ignored or explained away. Jesus had rebuked the two travelers on the way to Emmaus for believing only part of the Scriptures; and now, gathered with His disciples just before He was to leave them, He gives them once more the message, *believe all the Scriptures*. After Jesus had invited the disciples to handle Him and see and examine the wounds in His hands and feet, He then proved that He was indeed the resurrected *human* Jesus, and not a spirit, when He asked for food,

> And they gave him a piece of a broiled fish, and of an honeycomb.
> And he took it, and did eat before them (Luke 24: 42, 43).

Now notice what follows, for these are among the last words spoken by our Lord before He went to Heaven:

> And he [Jesus] said unto them, These are the words which I spake unto you, while I was yet with you, that all things must be fulfilled, which were written in the *law of Moses,* and *in the prophets,* and *in the psalms, concerning me.*
> Then opened he their understanding, that they might understand the scriptures,
> And said unto them, Thus it is written, and thus it behoved Christ to suffer, and to rise from the dead the third day (Luke 24:44-46).

WHY THE EMPHASIS?

Now the question might be raised, "Why all the emphasis on the rebuke of Jesus to His disciples for not believing *all the Scriptures?*" In a measure we can excuse the disciples for their ignorance and failure to see Jesus in all the Old Testament, beginning with Moses and all the prophets. How much more serious it is for us on this side of Calvary and Pentecost not to believe *all* that the Scriptures teach. We are living in an age of skepticism. The Scriptures have lost their air of authority for many Christians. The Bible is not held in respect by vast areas of the professing church. It is being twisted, revised, perverted, changed, and re-edited by self-appointed and irresponsible theologians, translators and revisers. There is today a swelling tide of denials of the Word of God, and much of the attack is leveled against the books of Moses. We are told that the story of creation, the fall, the Garden of Eden, and the Ark of Noah are just tradition and folklore. They are placed on a level with Aesop's fables and fairy tales. We are led to believe that the first part of the Bible is not historical fact and an actual, literal account of creation, the entrance of sin and redemption. We are told that if we believe this record literally, we reveal our ignorance. We are not scientific, and scholars have long since given up belief in the record of the Book of Genesis.

We have spent all this time in this chapter to show that it is impossible to accept part of the record and reject the remainder. If parts of the Bible are myth and other parts are true, then who is to be the judge to decide which is authentic and which is not? We repeat, it is either *all* or *nothing*. Jesus said that *all* the Scriptures spoke of Him. He believed the books of Moses. To deny the first part of the Bible is to destroy the whole.

No Excuse for Us

If Jesus rebuked the people of His generation for not believing *all* the Scriptures (Luke 24:25), then what excuse have we with the added light of the New Testament and the illumination of the Spirit of Pentecost? And yet the ignorance of the average believer concerning the Word of God is appalling and shocking. This may offend many of you, and be very unwelcome, but one of the most discouraging things in my ministry is to find that after teaching some people for years, they are still children as far as knowledge of the Word is concerned. I sometimes ask myself, "Where have I failed in my ministry? Why can people listen to my efforts at teaching week after week, and still remain so uninformed about the Word of God? Is it because people, like the disciples of old, accept only that which they like to hear, and reject the remainder?"

The purpose of the Radio Bible Class is not only to teach the Word of God, but also to interest men and women *personally* in a study of the Bible itself. But it does take *study*. It takes more than just repeating the Lord's Prayer and reciting the 23rd Psalm. Study means work! In these chapters we therefore seek not only to stir up within you a desire to know more of the Word, but also to help you to make it a delightful as well as a helpful exercise. In these lessons we shall try to show you how to find Jesus anywhere and everywhere in the Scriptures.

Without the light of the New Testament it would be impossible to recognize the various types, shadows, and pictures of Jesus in the Old Testament, but with the light of the New Testament, it is made easy if we are but willing to *search the Scriptures*. We have already seen Him in the opening verse of Genesis:

> In the beginning God created the heaven and the earth (Genesis 1:1).

In the light of the New Testament we know that this great God, the Creator, was none other than Jesus Christ, the Eternal Word, for John says plainly,

> All things were made by him; and without him was not any thing made that was made (John 1:3).

Then we see in Adam a type of the Lord Jesus, as His Bride was taken from His wounded side, and finally Adam is seen as the type of Jesus in His love for His Bride, saving her by His own death. In our next chapter we shall study the *first* mention of the Redeemer by name, and the *first* clear picture of Calvary in the Bible. It will greatly profit you if you will read carefully Genesis chapter 3, and see if you can find in it a clear picture of the One who said,

> Search the scriptures; for in them ye think ye have eternal life: and they are they which testify of me (John 5:39).

7

THE PROTEVANGELIUM

From Genesis to Revelation the Bible contains one unbroken testimony to the Lord Jesus Christ. He Himself said that all the Scriptures speak of Him (Luke 24:27). This, of course, includes the books of Moses which are under such relentless and vicious attack today. Jesus seemed to anticipate the time when so-called theological scholars would attack the first part of the Bible written by Moses, and so took special pains to emphasize His firm belief in the historicity and authenticity of the Pentateuch or the writings of Moses. He said in John 5:45-47,

> Do not think that I will accuse you to the Father: there is one that accuseth you, even Moses, in whom ye trust.
> For had ye believed Moses, ye would have believed me: for he wrote of me.
> But if ye believed not his writings, how shall ye believe my words?

We make no apologies for repeating these words of our Lord, for they make us face up squarely to the question, Was Jesus mistaken when He gave His unqualified endorsement to the writings of Moses? To reject the books of Moses is to reject Jesus Christ Himself. Yet, those who consider us stupid, and hold themselves up as intellectuals and scholars, openly repudiate the words of the Lord Jesus and still call themselves Christian.

59

WHAT THEY SAY

Yet these so-called intellectuals and scholarly theologians laugh at the literal interpretation of the Scriptures. They make the bold, wholly unsupported claim that the first five books of the Bible were composed by a dozen or more authors and written hundreds of years after Moses was supposed to have lived. They frankly assert that Moses was not a real person at all, but a fictitious person invented by these fraudulent writers. According to these scholars the books of Moses are simply a mythical and confused account of the origin of the people and institutions of Israel. The Books of Ruth and Esther are only romantic love stories, and are mere fiction. Most of these critics now deny that David wrote any of the Psalms. And this is being taught in many of our so-called Christian (?) colleges and seminaries and preached from many of our pulpits in the land.

EXCEPT A MAN BE BORN AGAIN

However, to the believer in Jesus Christ all this nonsense, while it may be disturbing, does not move us from our position of believing *all* the Scriptures. We repeat, it is either *all* or *nothing*. To the believer, the fact of the Lord Jesus is to be found on every page of Scripture plainly and unmistakably. How then are we to account for the inability of these highly educated scholars to see what the humblest child of God sees in the Bible? Jesus gives the explanation in His discourse with a highly intellectual and educated scholar by the name of Nicodemus. Here was a prominent leader in the nation of Israel, a real *brain* if there ever was one, and yet he was totally blind to spiritual matters. He asked of Jesus, "How can these things be?" and Jesus gives him the answer, "*Ye must be born again.*" Nicodemus with all his education and training was as blind as a bat, and so Jesus says,

> . . . Except a man be born again, he cannot *see* . . .
> (John 3:3).

He cannot *see.* He is blind to spiritual things, although he might be the brainiest, brightest genius in the realm of the natural. Have you ever wondered why some of the wisest of our scientists, astronomers, geologists, physiologists, biologists, doctors and teachers fail to see God's hand in all their investigations? It is simply because until a man is born again he is totally blind to spiritual matters. Paul states it most clearly when he writes to the Corinthians:

> But the natural man receiveth not the things of the Spirit of God: for they are foolishness unto him: neither can he know them, because they are spiritually discerned (I Corinthians 2:14).

And in II Corinthians, he makes this statement:

> But if our gospel be hid, it is hid to them that are lost: In whom the god of this world hath blinded the minds of them which believe not, lest the light of the glorious gospel of Christ, who is the image of God, should shine unto them (II Corinthians 4:3, 4).

Here then is the reason the simplest believer in Christ finds in the Bible a mine of precious jewels, while the most erudite and sophisticated unbeliever does not even see one glint of its glory.

In these messages on pictures of Christ in Genesis, we have no difficulty in finding all through the Old Testament, types, shadows, figures, and outlines of the Lord Jesus. We are often criticized for putting Jesus into some of the more obscure passages of the Bible. They accuse us of stretching our imagination in seeking for types and pictures of the Saviour in every passage of Scripture. But the fact that they do not see it, does not mean that we do not.

THE PROTEVANGELIUM

Now we are ready to proceed with more portraits of Christ in the Scriptures. We take up the *first* promise of the Redeemer in the Bible. It is found early in Genesis:

And I will put enmity between thee and the woman,
and between thy seed and her seed; it shall bruise thy
head, and thou shalt bruise his heel (Genesis 3:15).

This verse is known theologically as the *protevangelium*,
meaning the *first* promise of a coming Redeemer for fallen
man. Man had disobeyed God's command concerning the
forbidden fruit, and had come under sentence of death. Frantically Adam and Eve tried to hide from God and cover their
nakedness with the leaves of a fig tree. But it was all to no
avail, and so God came to the rescue with the promise of
hope. We remind you that this is an unmistakable prophecy
and picture of Christ the Redeemer. We point out a number of important facts in this first promise of redemption.

1. Notice first of all that this declaration of war and ultimate victory was spoken to the enemy, the serpent, and not
to Mother Eve. This verse, Genesis 3:15, serves notice on
Satan that although he seems to have won the first skirmish
against the Word of God, it is only the beginning of a conflict which will end in complete victory for the *Seed* of the
woman.

2. Notice next that this promise of victory was given soon
after the fall, and before Adam and Eve were banished from
the Garden. God had declared the sure penalty of death, both
physical and spiritual, upon their sin, and so before the poor
sinner could die and be lost forever, God came with the
glorious promise of redemption. What an illustration of the
words of Paul, that "where sin abounded, grace did much
more abound" (Romans 5:20).

3. Then, thirdly, notice that we have here the first clear
mention of the *Virgin Birth* of the Lord Jesus, here called the
seed of the woman. Every human being born since the days
of Adam and Eve is the seed of Adam. The seed is always
traced through the male line. But there is one exception to
this rule. Jesus Christ is called the "seed of the woman."
There is no mention of Adam in this verse at all, and this is

the one and only place in the entire Bible where a person is
called the "seed of the woman." It was Eve who fell before
the deception of Satan, and God has designed that the woman
too should bring forth the Redeemer. By woman had come
sin, and by woman should come the Saviour. By woman
had come the curse, and by woman should come the One
who would remove the curse. Yes, indeed, "where sin
abounded, grace did much more abound." The coming Saviour was to be virgin-born, without a human father. Higher
critics and skeptics have ridiculed the doctrine of the Virgin
Birth of Christ, and have attacked especially the verse in
Isaiah 7:14,

> . . . Behold, a virgin shall conceive, and bear a son,
> and shall call his name Immanuel.

All the attacks of the critics have concentrated on this verse,
because they say the Hebrew word "almah" may also refer
simply to a young woman. However, the New Testament
gives its real meaning in the account of the Virgin Birth of
Jesus (Matthew 1:23; Luke 1:27). But the revelation of the
Virgin Birth goes way back to the Garden of Eden where the
coming Deliverer is called the seed of the *woman,* not the
seed of the *man.*

4. Then notice further that there are two seeds mentioned,
the seed of the serpent and the seed of the woman. Since
the seed of the woman was to be a person, the seed of the
serpent will also be a person. Satan will have a personal seed
as well as the woman. These two seeds are later identified
as Christ and the Antichrist. Since Christ will be the supernatural Son of God, the Antichrist will reveal himself in the
end time as the *son of perdition,* the man of sin. The final
struggle announced in this first declaration of war in Genesis
3:15 will be between Christ, the Son of God, and the Antichrist, the son of perdition. That the seed of the serpent will
be a literal person is the only logical conclusion we can reach

in view of the fact that the seed of the woman will be the *personal Redeemer* — the Man, Christ Jesus.

5. One more observation we would make before we conclude this inexhaustible picture of the coming Deliverer in the Protevangelium of Genesis 3:15. And this final observation is of utmost importance if we are to understand the age-long struggle between the seed of the woman and the seed of the serpent until the final victory of the end time. In Genesis 3:15 we have the beginning of the "battle of the seeds" between Satan and Christ. It will be finally culminated in the complete victory of the Saviour. We have the account of this final victory in the last book of the Bible. It begins in Genesis and ends in Revelation. The personal Antichrist is defeated and cast into the lake of fire at the Second Coming of Christ (Revelation 19:20), while Satan himself will be doomed to the same place later on (Revelation 20:10).

Between these two events (the beginning of the battle in Genesis 3, and the end of the battle in Revelation 20) is a history of struggle which indeed seems to be in favor of the enemy, for will you notice we have two *bruisings* in this verse. The seed of the serpent will bruise the heel of the seed of the woman, and ultimately the seed of the woman will bruise the head of the serpent. One of these bruisings is history — when the Redeeemer came the first time it seemed to be a victory for the enemy, for the Redeemer was put to death on the cross. Here His heel was bruised, symbolic of the sufferings and death of our Saviour, who was "wounded for our transgressions, and *bruised* for our iniquities" (Isaiah 53:5). This part of the promise and prediction of Genesis 3:15 is history. It happened almost two thousand years ago, but it was only His heel which was bruised. The other "bruising" of the serpent's head is still future. It will be consummated at the Second Coming of Christ. The Saviour's heel was bruised at His First Coming, but Satan's head will be crushed at His Second Coming. This is the only possible interpretation of the prediction of Genesis 3:15.

We must emphasize the difference between the two "bruisings," not only as to time but also result. The bruising of the heel was not fatal, but the bruising of the head *is fatal*. It will be the end of Satan's attack upon both the Redeemer and His redeemed. It will take place when our Lord returns to earth in person and power, and when "the dragon, that old serpent, which is the Devil, and Satan, shall be bound for a thousand years, and be cast into the bottomless pit" (Revelation 20:2, 3).

Evidence of Inspiration

What an evidence of the divine inspiration of the Word of God! Who but He who knoweth the end from the beginning could have given such an accurate, unassailable outline of all subsequent history and condensed it all within the limits of one verse of only twenty-eight words, way back in the Garden of Eden? One wonders indeed how the skeptics and unbelievers can fail to see in this one verse alone the incontrovertible evidence of divine inspiration. What human mind could have conceived such a prediction? It is only because the same "mastermind" who deceived the woman in the Garden is still blinding the eyes of them that believe not. But all these attacks upon the Word do not disturb us who believe, when we have such evidence of divine revelation and the witness of the Spirit of God through this infallible Word.

If you cannot see in all this God's revelation of His Son, then you are still blinded by unbelief. The Bible needs no proof; it needs only to be honestly faced and believed. Then every page of the Book will reveal a picture of the Christ of God.

8

THREE REQUIREMENTS IN SACRIFICE

The Old Testament is a book of shadows. From Genesis to Malachi it contains shadows of the coming Redeemer, the central figure of the Bible. Paul says that the record of the Old Testament under the law was

> . . . a shadow of things to come; but the body is of Christ (Colossians 2:17).

The dictionary defines a shadow as the "deprivation of light representing on a surface the forms of the body which intercepts the rays of light, a faint representation or a typical representation." A shadow must have light, and it must have an object. The object cuts off the light and casts a shadow which more or less faintly corresponds to the body which casts the shadow. The object of the Old Testament revelation which casts its shadow is Jesus Christ. Paul says that the Old Testament was a shadow of things to come, but the body is Christ. The distinctiveness or clarity of the shadow depends upon the angle at which the light strikes the body. For instance, I stand in the sunlight early in the morning just after sunrise. The shadow my body casts is entirely out of proportion. It stretches across the lawn, across the road, and disappears in the field of grass beyond. The shadow reveals nothing more than that there is a body intercepting the light. However, as the sun rises higher the shadow becomes shorter and more distinct and begins to approximate the shape and size of the body which casts the shadow. At mid-forenoon, at an angle of forty-five degrees, the shadow will be the same size as the body, and begin to reveal accurate details and features not visible before. As the sun reaches its zenith at high noon the shadow disappears and only the body is visible. So it is with the progressive revelation of the Bible. When the sun of revelation began to shine way back in Genesis, there were shadows of things to come, but they were dim and faint; and without more light they were entirely indistinguishable. We are familiar with the saying, "Coming events cast their shadows before," and this is true of the Bible. At first it is impossible to identify the body which casts the shadow. As more light appears the body comes into view, so that when Jesus came nineteen hundred years ago, the shadows departed in the brightness of Him who is the Light of the World. Now with the full light of the New Testament we easily recognize Christ in all the shadows, types and figures of prophecy.

Progressive Revelation

Today, with the revelation of Christ complete, we see a shadow and picture of Christ in the very first verse of the Bible, "In the beginning God created." This Creator God, we saw in an earlier chapter, was Jesus Christ Himself (John 1:3). Then we saw a slightly more detailed shadow in the creation of Adam's bride from his wounded side, and again we recognized the picture of Jesus. The light increased and we saw Adam as a type of the Lord Jesus in His love for His bride (so great that He was willing to die in her stead); and then in our last message we saw a beautiful picture of Christ in the Seed of the Woman, promised in Genesis 3:15.

More Detail Added

In this same chapter (Genesis 3) we have added light thrown on this promised seed and the shadow becomes an unmistakable picture of how this Redeemer seed will accomplish His wonderful salvation. It is found in Genesis 3:21, and has been described as the first clear gospel sermon preached by God Himself. The verse should be familiar:

> Unto Adam also and to his wife did the LORD God make coats of skins, and clothed them (Genesis 3:21).

In this verse so early in human history we have God's inviolable requirement for the sinner's salvation. It is the first totally clear revelation of Calvary. Before looking at the indescribably rich teaching of this verse, we must mention the setting. Man had disobeyed God and was under sentence of death. Adam and Eve were conscious of their predicament, but sin had so blinded their eyes that instead of fleeing to God for help, they frantically tried to effect their own salvation. They imagined that they could *do* something to make them once more presentable to God. Before man fell, he was clothed in the garments of innocence, but no sooner had he sinned than he lost this covering and discovered that he was shamefully naked. The Bible says,

> And the eyes of them both were opened, and they knew that they were naked; and they sewed fig leaves together, and made themselves aprons (Genesis 3:7).

However, the fig-leaf aprons were wholly inadequate and might just as well have been poison ivy. Now Adam and Eve knew deep down in their hearts that their aprons were wholly inadequate, for if they had believed this covering was sufficient they would not have continued to hide from the Lord.

THE LORD TO THE RESCUE

While Adam and Eve were hiding from God, the Lord was seeking them. What a demonstration of grace, and that "where sin abounded, grace did much more abound" (Romans 5:20). The Lord utterly rejected their vain efforts to cover up their guilt, and we read in our text this glorious, inexhaustible, marvelous message of redemption and grace:

Unto Adam also and to his wife did the LORD God
make coats of skins, and clothed them (Genesis 3:21).

It would take volumes to teach all of the precious truths in
this early picture of God's provision for the fallen sinner
through the sacrifice of Christ, and we can point out only
a few lessons.

PATTERN FOR ALL SALVATION

As God took a sacrificial animal (probably a lamb) and
slew it before Adam's eyes, and wrapped the bloody skins
about his naked body, God laid down an eternal, divine principle from which there is no deviation. In this act of God
He laid down three inviolable rules of acceptable atonement
for sin.

1. The first thing to notice in this first record of an acceptable sacrifice is that it is all done by God. The animal was
God's gift and not the work of man. How beautiful and unmistakable is the type of our Lord Jesus — the perfect Lamb
of God. It was the Lord alone who furnished the skins to
cover Adam and Eve. They did nothing, absolutely nothing.
The only sacrifice God would accept must be God's work and
God's free gift. Our first parents did not even have to put
the coats of skins on themselves. Even this was done by God,
for we read that God "clothed them."

2. Secondly, notice from this first sacrifice that atonement
must be by the death of an innocent substitute. The animal
God slew to provide the skins had no part in Adam's sin. It
was an innocent victim. Man could not atone for his own
sin, for its penalty had been declared,

. . . in the day that thou eatest thereof thou shalt surely
die (Genesis 2:17).

If one single day had passed without this provision of a
substitute they would have died on the very day they fell.
So before that first day was ended, God came to them with

the message of redemption. On the evening of the very day Adam sinned God came with His substitutionary lamb. The record clearly suggests this, for we read that after Adam and his wife had hid themselves and were busy making the flimsy fig-leaf aprons, God came in the evening of the selfsame day to deliver them. It was in the "cool of the day," in the evening before that day ended that God came to them (Genesis 3:8).

3. Thirdly, notice that this atonement must be by the *shedding of blood*. While blood is not mentioned in the record, it is implied, for God could not procure the skins of the substitute without putting it to death and shedding its blood.

Also, notice the difference in God's covering and Adam's attempt. Adam's covering for his nakedness and sin are called *aprons* of fig leaves. God's covering is called "coats of skins." The Hebrew word for aprons is *khagore* and can be translated "a belt," while the word for robe is *kethoneth* and signifies a complete covering from head to foot. The same word is used for the high priestly robe which covered the whole body.

GOD'S PERFECT PATTERN

We repeat once more the three elements of an acceptable atoning sacrifice:

1. It must be God's gift, and His work alone.
2. It must be by the death of an innocent substitute.
3. It must be by the shedding of blood.

This then is God's initial declaration of the one and only acceptable sacrifice for sin which God will receive. Where one or more of these elements is missing it must be rejected by God. From this point on we can trace the doctrine of substitutionary atonement by blood throughout the entire Scripture. Where these conditions are met, God accepts the provision; where any part of this is missing, God must reject it. We have an illustration of it in the very next chapter (Genesis 4). Adam and Eve had two sons, Cain and Abel. These boys had evidently been instructed by Adam concerning the coat of skins and its provisions. Where else did these boys receive their information concerning God's requirements of sacrifice? Both these boys were religious and believed in God. Cain seemed to be the most religious of the two, for it was he who first thought of bringing an offering unto the Lord. The religion of Cain is briefly stated:

> . . . Cain brought of the fruit of the ground an offering unto the Lord (Genesis 4:3).

Cain was sincere, he was very religious, and felt he must do something to atone for his sin. Remember Cain brought an offering *unto the Lord*. But God would have nothing of it, and we read:

> But unto Cain and to his offering he [God] had not respect . . . (Genesis 4:5).

Why did God reject Cain's offering? Simply because he ignored God's rules, taught by the coats of skins. Cain's first mistake was that he brought of the "fruit of the ground," the result of his own labors, the work of his own hands, instead of a lamb, the gift of God. Secondly, Cain's offering did not involve the death of an innocent substitutionary victim. Thirdly, there was no shedding of blood, and "without shedding of blood there is no remission." So God rejected Cain's sincere, earnest religion of works. On the other hand, God accepted Abel's offering, for we read:

> And Abel, he also brought of the firstlings of his flock and of the fat thereof. And the Lord had respect unto Abel and to his offering (Genesis 4:4).

Why respect Abel's offering? Simply because he fulfilled God's requirements for an acceptable atonement:
1. He brought a lamb (a firstling of the flock).
2. He put it to death upon the altar; and
3. It was by the shedding of blood.
Just how God indicated His acceptance of Abel's sacrifice

and the rejection of Cain's we are not told, but it was probably by sending fire from Heaven to ignite the sacrifice of Abel. At least this was the way God showed His favor upon acceptable sacrifice later on (see Leviticus 9:24; I Kings 18: 38; II Chronicles 7:1).

These conditions laid down in the Garden of Eden are inviolable. Wherever conditions are met, God accepts the sacrifice; where they are violated, He rejects them. In this connection think of Abraham's sacrifice on Mt. Moriah. Or take the Passover. It was God's gift, a lamb; it must die; and the blood must be sprinkled on the lintel and the door posts. Follow this principle anywhere in the Bible, in the offerings of Israel, and all the sacrifices of the Old Testament.

And then finally the shadows disappear and the One to whom all this pointed appears on the scene. In the fullness of time God sent forth His Son, and He was proclaimed by John the Baptist as "the Lamb of God which taketh away the sin of the world." And He met all the requirements of that first clear picture of Him in Genesis 3:21.

1. He was God's free gift — "For God so loved the world that he *gave* his only begotten Son." The fig leaves of law-works would not suffice.

2. He must die as a substitute for sinners, and this He did, for Paul says:

> For if, when we were enemies, we were reconciled to God by the *death* of his Son, much more, being reconciled, we shall be saved by his life (Romans 5:10).

3. Finally, redemption through Christ must be by the shedding of His blood. Peter says,

> Forasmuch as ye know that ye were not redeemed with corruptible things, . . .
> But with the precious blood of Christ, as of a lamb without blemish and without spot (I Peter 1:18, 19).

All this was foreshadowed and promised in the first acceptable sacrifice recorded way back in the dawn of human history:

> Unto Adam also and to his wife did the Lord God make coats of skins, and clothed them (Genesis 3:21).

Oh, the blindness and stupidity of unbelief! How can anyone fail to see in this act of God the whole story of redemption? In the light of the New Testament this picture of Christ in Genesis 3:21 leaves no one with any excuse. God has etched the face of Christ upon every page of Holy Writ, if only we will allow the Holy Spirit to open our blind eyes to the glorious revelation of Jesus Christ.

9

CAIN, THE TYPE OF ISRAEL

> For by grace are ye saved through faith; and that not
> of yourselves: it is the gift of God:
> Not of works, lest any man should boast.
> For we are his workmanship . . . (Ephesians 2:8-10).

If there is one doctrine in the Bible which is crystal clear, it is the doctrine of "justification by faith, without the works of the law." Salvation is all of grace, and excludes every bit of human works or effort. This was the first lesson God taught fallen man after he had sinned. Adam tried by the work of his own hands to cover his nakedness, but God came, rejected his fig-leaf apron of works, and then proceeded to provide a salvation of grace, by taking a lamb, killing it, shedding its blood, and then covering man with the bloody skins of the slain animal.

To the spiritually enlightened believer this is an unmistakable picture of our Lord Jesus Christ who was "wounded for our transgressions, and bruised for our iniquities." In the very dawn of human history the Lord laid down the principle that "salvation is of the Lord," and that human works have no part or value in redemption. Soon after man was driven out of the Garden the Holy Spirit records another incident to drive home the truth of "salvation by grace through faith." It is the account of Cain and Abel and their sacrifices. Cain brought of the fruit of his own labor and was rejected. Abel presented God's offering in the sacrifice of an innocent substitutionary lamb and was accepted.

ONLY TWO RELIGIONS

In the case of Cain and Abel, we are brought face to face with the fact that there are only two religions in the world — a true and a false. We distinguish between many, many religions: Christianity, Buddhism, Mohammedanism, etc; and we divide Christianity into Presbyterian, Baptist, Reformed, Lutheran, Episcopalian, etc. But these are merely human classifications. With God there are only two: (1) a religion of works; and (2) a salvation by grace. Every church or denomination or religious group which teaches that man has anything at all to do with obtaining or earning or meriting his salvation is a false religion, regardless of its denominational or sectarian name. It is the religion of fig leaves and the offering of Cain. On the other hand, those who teach that men are totally lost, completely impotent to save themselves, and therefore must look to the work of God exclusively, are the recipients of true salvation under whatever name they may be known. Satan deceived Adam and Cain, making them feel they could do something to be saved, or at least help God a little bit in the work. But God refused to recognize it and provided salvation by grace.

Satan has not changed his method since then, but is still deceiving and causing people to believe they can please God by human works and efforts. Salvation by grace is a humiliating message to bring. Man will admit he is sick and needs some help, but tell him he is "dead" in trespasses and in sins and totally depraved and he will be insulted. Yet, until a person is willing to admit that he cannot do anything, but must rely completely on the grace of God, he cannot be saved. How many sing the well-known hymn without realizing the deep truth of its message:

Not the labors of my hands
Can fulfil thy law's demands;
Could my zeal no respite know,
Could my tears forever flow,
All for sin could not atone;
Thou must save, and Thou alone.

This then was the fundamental lesson on salvation the Lord revealed to our first parents back in Genesis 3. How clear is the picture of the coming One who was to be God's Lamb provided for sinners helpless to save themselves. How blind can men be, that they fail to see in all this God's revelation of His dear Son. No wonder Satan so relentlessly and persistently attacks the first few books of the Bible, and especially the Book of Genesis. As we see these pictures of Christ in this first book of the Bible, we can see through the Devil's scheme of attack, for once he has disproved the Book of Genesis, the whole structure of redemption falls to the ground. Genesis is the very rock foundation of God's redemptive program. Disprove the Book of Genesis, and we are left without an answer to the creation of the universe, the cause of death, and the presence of sin. And without the record of Genesis as to the beginning of sin, the cause of death, and God's provision, we are left without an answer to every problem of life. If Genesis is not true, then where did sin originate? How shall we explain sickness, diseases, suffering, warfare, violence, bloodshed and death? The Book of Genesis gives us the only answer. Let the infidels and unbelievers who deny the record of Genesis give us an explanation for the condition of the world, the evil heart of man, his sufferings, and agonies, and heartbreak, and finally death. And don't give us the silly drivel of a Pandora's box. If the record of Genesis be only a myth, then let them come up with a more logical myth than the account of Moses.

ABEL IS A PICTURE OF CHRIST

Before we leave the story of Cain and Abel, we must point out that Abel himself was a picture of the Lord Jesus Christ.

Not only was the acceptable sacrifice he presented to God an unmistakable picture of the Saviour meeting all the conditions laid down by God in Genesis 3:21, but Abel himself foreshadowed the coming seed who would be rejected and slain by his brethren because of his faithfulness to his God. In the story of Cain and Abel we have a shadow of God's dispensational program for the nation foreshadowed by Cain who slew his brother Abel. The Apostle John in commenting on this says in his first epistle:

> For this is the message that ye heard from the beginning, that we should love one another.
> Not as Cain, who was of that wicked one, and slew his brother. And wherefore slew he him? Because his own works were evil, and his brother's righteous (I John 3:11, 12).

The light of the New Testament leaves no doubt in our minds that all this was a type of the rejection and crucifixion of the Greater than Abel, and the subsequent judgment upon the ones who rejected Him. The Bible clearly says,

> Now all these things happened unto them for ensamples [types]: and they are written for our admonition [instruction] . . . (I Corinthians 10:11).

Abel then becomes a picture, a type of Christ who satisfied God's demands for a perfect sacrifice, but was rejected for it by His brethren. Abel was the first shepherd in history, and therefore immediately points us to Him who said, "I am the good shepherd: the good shepherd giveth his life for the sheep" (John 10:11). Abel died a violent death, and the shedding of his blood called for judgment. We quote here the simple record as given in Genesis 4, and I am sure you will be able to see the striking parallel between the death of Abel and the crucifixion and death of the Great Shepherd foreshadowed by Abel. After the slaying of Abel we read:

> And the LORD said unto Cain, Where is Abel thy brother?

> And he said, I know not: Am I my brother's keeper?
> And he said, What hast thou done? the voice of thy brother's blood crieth unto me from the ground.
> And now art thou cursed from the earth [land], which hath opened her mouth to receive thy brother's blood from thy hand;
> When thou tillest the ground, it shall not henceforth yield unto thee her strength; a fugitive and a vagabond shalt thou be in the earth (Genesis 4:9-12).

All this was a prophecy in type of what happened at Calvary. Here the Shepherd of Israel came to redeem His people, but the nation refused His offer and out of envy delivered Him up to be slain (Matthew 27:18). As a result the nation came under the judgment of God. The blood of their Brother cried from the ground in answer to their own words, "His blood be on us, and on our children" (Matthew 27:25). The judgment of God was revealed in the cursing of the land. God cursed Cain's farm so he was forced to abandon agriculture (his first occupation) and was driven to city life instead. All this was fulfilled in the land of Canaan which, described as a land of corn and wine, of milk and honey, became a barren wilderness. All of this was prophesied beforehand. Moses wrote in Leviticus 26:32,

> And I will bring the land into desolation: and your enemies which dwell therein shall be astonished at it.

All this is implied in the type of Cain when God drove him from the land. Cain was driven out of the land and became a fugitive and a wanderer in the earth. All this too had been predicted, and prophesied:

> And I will scatter you among the heathen [Gentiles], and will draw out a sword after you: and your land shall be desolate, and your cities waste (Leviticus 26:33).

Driven from the land, Cain went and dwelt in the land of Nod (Genesis 4:16). The expression, "land of Nod," means land of "wandering." He now became a city dweller instead of a farmer.

> And Cain went out from the presence of the LORD, and dwelt in the land of Nod [wandering], . . .
> . . . and he builded a city, and called the name of the city, after the name of his son, Enoch (Genesis 4:16,17).

GOD'S ETERNAL PLAN

For these past two thousand years the Promised Land has been abandoned. Just recently a part of it has been restored to the nation of Israel, but the great majority of Jews are still scattered throughout the world. Here among the nations they are the objects of God's special care and protection. After God had pronounced judgment on Cain, he replied:

> Behold, thou hast driven me out this day from the face of the earth [land]; and from thy face shall I be hid; and I shall be a fugitive and a vagabond in the earth; and it shall come to pass, that every one that findeth me shall slay me (Genesis 4:14).

Fear gripped the heart of Cain, and everyone seemed to be his enemy. Despairingly he said, "Every one that findeth me shall slay me." All this was a prophecy of the history of the nation represented by Cain during the centuries of their dispersion and persecution among the nations. We have but to remember the pogroms of history, some so recent in Germany and other countries, that except for the protection of God, the nation would long ago have been exterminated. But God is a God of great grace and He now comes to the defense of guilty Cain, and we read these remarkable words:

> And the LORD said unto him, Therefore whosoever slayeth Cain, vengeance shall be taken on him sevenfold. And the LORD set a mark upon Cain, lest any finding him should kill him (Genesis 4:15).

Amazing, wonderful, indescribable grace! Undeserving Cain now became the object of God's supernatural preservation. He marked him out as the object of His special protection. One need hardly point out the fulfillment of this type in the supernatural preservation of the scattered nation of

Israel. In grace He will keep them, and when His great program of redemption draws to a close, Israel shall be redeemed, restored back to her land, and become the head of the nations. This is *sovereign grace*. God promised to protect and preserve Cain, and He kept His word. So too God has promised in His everlasting covenant with Abraham, Isaac and Jacob, that His seed would remain forever, and in His seed all nations of the earth would be blessed.

> For I would not, brethren, that ye should be ignorant of this mystery, lest ye should be wise in your own conceits; that blindness in part is happened to Israel, until the fulness of the Gentiles be come in.
> And so all Israel shall be saved: as it is written, There shall come out of Sion the Deliverer, and shall turn away ungodliness from Jacob (Romans 11:25, 26).

10

THE GOD-PLANNED ARK

> By faith Noah, being warned of God of things not
> seen as yet, moved with fear, prepared an ark to the
> saving of his house; by the which he condemned the
> world, and became heir of the righteousness which is
> by faith (Hebrews 11:7).

Noah was saved because he had faith in the word of God
concerning an ark whereby he and his family would be
saved. We are saved in the very same way, by faith in God's
Word concerning His Son Jesus Christ, our Saviour from
the coming judgment, of which the Flood was a picture and
type. One cannot fail to see, therefore, in the Ark of Noah a
shadow, a type, of the coming Redeemer, the Lord Jesus
Christ. It is another of the innumerable portraits and pictures of Christ so lavishly scattered throughout the entire
Old Testament, and especially in the books of Moses, and
more especially in the Book of Genesis. We emphasize the
frequent pictures of Christ in the Book of Genesis because
of the special attack by critics and unbelievers on this particular book of the Bible. God must have anticipated the
modern attack upon this first book of the Bible, and so has
guarded it with so many pictures and types of coming events
that there is no excuse for anyone's not accepting it as the
infallible revelation of God. No one can be saved who denies
the authenticity and genuineness of the Book of Genesis.

That statement can bear repetition. There is no salvation possible for that individual who does not accept and believe the Book of Genesis as literally inspired, and a historical account of its contents. If Genesis be a myth, then Jesus who endorsed it becomes a myth as well. But to the spiritually enlightened mind the evidence is overwhelming and convincing as we have seen in earlier chapters. We pass on now to the typology of the Ark of Noah as a picture of the Lord Jesus Christ. We shall be able to point out only a few of the many points in which the Ark of Noah was a picture of the coming Christ.

Planned by God

The very first thing to notice is that the idea of an ark for the preservation of Noah and his family originated in the heart of God. It was not the invention of man. It was not because Noah, alarmed by the increasing wickedness of man, perceived that judgment was impending, and therefore sought for a plan whereby he might be spared in the imminent catastrophe. There is no hint that Noah anticipated a flood. There had evidently been no rain up until this time, and so the idea of a deluge was as far from Noah's mind as anything could possibly be. Before the Flood came or instructions were given to Noah to build an ark, the idea for the salvation of Noah and his family already existed in the mind of God. He foreknew the wickedness of man in the antediluvian days, and also knew that He would send the judgment upon the world. But in His wrath God remembered Noah, and He planned for his safety beforehand.

As the Ark was planned by God, and God alone, so too the antitype of the Ark, the Lord Jesus Christ, was foreordained by God to meet the judgment of sin (typified by the Flood), and to make provision for the safety of the elect. Peter tells us in speaking of Christ the Lamb of God,

Who verily was foreordained before the foundation
of the world, but was manifest in these last times for
you (I Peter 1:20).

And in Revelation 13 He is called "the Lamb slain from
the foundation of the world" (Revelation 13:8).

Not only was the Ark designed and planned by God in
every detail, but Noah and his family were also planned for,
long before they were even born. Paul says of us, who are
represented by Noah,

Blessed be the God and Father of our Lord Jesus
Christ, who hath blessed us with all spiritual blessings
in heavenly places in Christ:

According as he hath chosen us in him before the
foundation of the world, that we should be holy and
without blame before him in love:

Having predestinated us unto the adoption of children by Jesus Christ to himself, according to the good
pleasure of his will,

In whom also we have obtained an inheritance, being
predestinated according to the purpose of him who
worketh all things after the counsel of his own will
(Ephesians 1:3-5, 11).

It Is All of Grace

Noah had no part in the planning of this mighty ship.
All the blueprints and specifications were furnished by God.
It was *all* the work of God, and man had no hand in it at
all. Now all this is in harmony with the lessons we saw in
the coats of skins, Abel's sacrifice, and God's provision for
man's salvation. Not a detail is overlooked. Man must have
no part in the plan of salvation. How wonderful, therefore,
that after we read:

And God saw that the wickedness of man was great
in the earth . . .

And the LORD said, I will destroy man whom I have
created from the face of the earth; . . . (Genesis 6:5, 7),

the Word goes on to say in verse 8,

But Noah found grace in the eyes of the LORD.

In every picture of Christ in these early chapters in Genesis we encounter the cardinal truth of grace. It was so when God rejected man's work of fig-leaf aprons; it was so when God rejected Cain's works and saved Abel by grace. Noah alone and his family were chosen to escape the universal judgment of God, but it was not because Noah deserved it; it was still by *grace.*

SUPERNATURAL REVELATION

Notice further, in addition to the fact that the Ark was entirely a product of the mind of God, that it called for a supernatural revelation in order to reveal it to the heart of Noah. And so God gave a divine revelation concerning the coming judgment:

> And God said unto Noah, The end of all flesh is come before me; for the earth is filled with violence through them; and, behold, I will destroy them with the earth (Genesis 6:13).

God announced judgment upon sin, but no sooner had He pronounced the sentence than He also gave a plan of escape from the judgment. The same was true of Adam and Eve, for in the very day they sinned and came under judgment, God revealed His plan of salvation by the sacrifice of a lamb, in providing our parents with a covering of bloody skins. It was so in the case of Noah. Scarcely had God pronounced judgment when He revealed a plan of escape, and so the record continues in verse 14:

> Make thee an ark of gopher wood; rooms shalt thou make in the ark, and shalt pitch it within and without with pitch (Genesis 6:14).

Then notice the details given by God for the building of this Ark. Not a single thing is left up to man; the whole plan is of God. He says:

> And this is the fashion which thou shalt make it of: The length of the ark shall be three hundred cubits

[450 feet], the breadth of it fifty cubits [75 feet], and the height of it thirty cubits [45 feet] (Genesis 6:15).

Incidentally, modern shipbuilders tell us these dimensions are the most ideal measurements to ensure the safest and most seaworthy craft. The Ark was built on dry land, miles from the nearest water. Noah had no model to work from, and yet the Ark had the ideal dimensions for a ship accepted by shipbuilders even today. What an evidence of divine inspiration! No human mind could have conceived such a structure without the knowledge of a similar one. But, as we said, this Ark was designed and planned by the all-wise Creator. Let infidels explain how Noah could devise such a perfectly proportioned ship four to five thousand years ago, when he himself probably had never before seen a rowboat or a canoe. Yes, the whole plan of the Ark was supernaturally revealed to Noah by the One who gave all the details. And Noah believed what God said about the Ark. In Hebrews 11:7 we read:

> By faith Noah, being warned of God of things not seen as yet, moved with fear, prepared an ark to the saving of his house; by the which he condemned the world, and became heir of the righteousness which is by faith.

Noah believed what God told him about the Flood and the Ark, although there was no evidence of either. He just believed God's word. Now don't forget that the Ark is a type of the Lord Jesus Christ, our only hope against the judgment of God. And He too must be accepted by faith. All we have is the Word of God concerning Jesus Christ, and it is by believing that Word we are saved. With Peter we must say:

> Whom having not seen, ye love; in whom, though now ye see him not, yet believing, ye rejoice with joy unspeakable and full of glory (I Peter 1:8).

It was the same in the days of Noah. He was warned of things "not seen as yet." God announced the coming of something which had never been seen before; namely, *rain* from Heaven. Evidently before the Flood there had never been any rain. At least there is no mention of it, but the Word says that

> . . . God had not caused it to rain upon the earth, . . .
> But there went up a mist from the earth, and watered
> the whole face of the ground (Genesis 2:5, 6).

The ground before the Flood was watered by a mist or dew so heavy that "it watered the whole face of the ground." All the moisture came *up* from below — *nothing* from up above. And now God announces a flood, a deluge. Water was now to come *down* from Heaven as well as from the ground. Unbelievable! It had never happened before, but God said it would, and Noah believed it. This is the meaning of the words in Hebrews 11:7, "Noah, being warned of God of things not seen as yet [never seen before]." Just as Noah had nothing else to base his faith on than the word of God, so we today must receive Jesus Christ only on the authority of the Word of God. We cannot prove the existence of Jesus Christ in Heaven except by the record of this Book — the Bible. It must be received by faith.

BELIEVE THE RECORD

John tells us in I John 5,

> If we receive the witness of men, the witness of God is greater: for this is the witness of God which he hath testified of his Son.
> He that believeth on the Son of God hath the witness in himself: he that believeth not God hath made him a liar; because he believeth not the record that God gave of his Son (I John 5:9, 10).

Salvation is believing the record God gave of His Son, and acting upon it. It was no different with Noah. He had nothing to go on but the word of God, but he believed it, acted upon it, and was saved. There is only one way of salvation, and this is by faith in the Word of God concerning

His Son Jesus Christ. In the Old Testament, the age of shadows, men were saved no differently. It was always by faith in the word of God, and from the New Testament we know that Jesus is the *Word*. When the Old Testament saint believed what God said, whether it be Adam, Abel, Noah or Abraham, it was really faith in Jesus Christ who is the eternal Word of God.

ONLY ONE DOOR

Returning for a moment again to the Ark as a most complete type of the Lord Jesus Christ, we remind you once more that man had no part in its planning. The Lord gave all the details for its construction. The description, brief but complete, continues in Genesis 6,

> A window shalt thou make to the ark, and in a cubit shalt thou finish it above; and the door of the ark shalt thou set in the side thereof; with lower, second, and third stories shalt thou make it (Genesis 6:16).

Time permits us merely to mention the details of the *door*. A number of unusual features are seen. First, there is *only one door*. Today such an arrangement would not be allowed. A building of this size would have to have several exits, and be equipped with life rafts, lifeboats and life preservers for its passengers. But none of these things is mentioned, for they were completely unnecessary. As we shall see, God had provided for the *perfect* safety of the occupants, for God was Himself with them in the ship. There was no need for any safety features within the Ark, for it was a type of Jesus the Christ, and just as God was with Noah in the ship, so "God was *in Christ* reconciling the world to himself."

One final thought, and a strange one! The dimensions of the door are not mentioned. We don't know how high or how wide it was. This was for a definite reason. Since no dimensions are given, all can gain entrance. No matter how great a sinner one may be, there is room for him through Him who said, *"I am the door."*

11

SAFE IN THE ARK

Never before in history has there been such a relentless, destructive attack upon the Bible as in these last days. The chief point of attack is the Pentateuch, the five books of Moses, and among these the Book of Genesis is singled out for this onslaught by infidels and skeptics. The teaching widely disseminated even in our Sunday schools and churches is that Genesis has no historical basis, and that it is not an accurate or literal account of the creation of the earth and man, of the entrance of sin and of the early history of Abraham. It is characterized as entirely mythical, on a level with pagan mythology, fables and folklore. Two of the areas being most viciously attacked in recent days are the account of the Flood of Noah as recorded in Genesis chapters 6 to 9; and the record of the destruction of Sodom and Gomorrah as recorded in Genesis 19. Yet it was these two events which Jesus singled out to indicate what He thought of the account in the Book of Genesis.

The Lord knew beforehand that these two records, the Flood and the destruction of Sodom, would be called in question by the critics in these latter days, and so He goes out of His way to place His seal of endorsement upon these two accounts. He leaves no doubt about the matter at all. He says in Luke 17,

And as it was in the days of Noe, so shall it be also in the days of the Son of man.

They did eat, they drank, they married wives, they were given in marriage, until the day that Noe entered into the ark, and the flood came, and destroyed them all (Luke 17:26, 27).

Did Jesus believe the record of Genesis concerning Noah and the Flood? If He didn't He certainly practiced a colossal bit of deception and is unworthy of any respect or confidence. Let the skeptics find an answer. Of course, they would even dare to suggest that Jesus was mistaken, and didn't know any better. And how about the miracle of the destruction of Sodom and Gomorrah? How about Lot's wife having been turned into a pillar of salt? Listen to what Jesus thought about this. He says in Luke 17,

Likewise also as it was in the days of Lot; they did eat, they drank, they bought, they sold, they planted, they builded:

But the same day that Lot went out of Sodom it rained fire and brimstone from heaven, and destroyed them all.

Even thus shall it be in the day when the Son of man is revealed.

Remember Lot's wife (Luke 17:28-30, 32).

The Virgin Birth

We repeat, therefore, that the Scriptures from Genesis to Revelation were given with the primary purpose of revealing Jesus Christ, the Son of God and the Son of man. Every part of the revelation has some bearing on His person, character and mission. Even those passages in the Bible which record the atrocities, the slaughters of men, the immorality and the violence of men and nations, are recorded to show the need of salvation and the hopeless depravity of the natural human heart. In our previous study we began an examination of the Ark of Noah as a picture and a portrait of Jesus Christ, the Saviour from judgment. The wickedness of man had become so great in the days before the Flood that God said,

> . . . My spirit shall not always strive with man, for that he also is flesh: yet his days shall be an hundred and twenty years.
>
> And God saw that the wickedness of man was great in the earth, and that every imagination of the thoughts of his heart was only evil continually.
>
> And the LORD said, I will destroy man whom I have created from the face of the earth; . . . (Genesis 6:3, 5, 7).

After God had revealed His plan of salvation in the slaying of the substitutionary lamb in Genesis 3:21 to provide a covering of skins for Adam and Eve, the world did not accept the lesson, and things did not begin to get better and better. Instead they became worse and worse. And so God commanded Noah to build an ark of salvation for a remnant of mankind. The Ark was the only escape.

Jesus used this historic incident to illustrate the condition of the world just prior to His Second Coming. According to the Bible the world will not become better and better during this age, but instead worse and worse. Without the intervention of God, man would ultimately destroy himself. This age will not see the world brought to Christ, it will not culminate in a blaze of glory with world-wide revival. There is not one verse in the entire Bible to indicate a great turning to God before the return of Jesus for His Church. Not only do we have abundant Bible passages to show that this age will end in apostasy (and who is so blind as not to see it today in this ecumenical deluge of compromise), but Jesus by referring us to the days *before the Flood,* shows us a pattern which will be followed just before the return of Jesus *for His Church.*

It will be the same Jesus so plainly foreshadowed by the Ark of Noah. In our last chapter we pointed out the unmistakable figure of the Ark as pointing to Jesus, by calling your attention to the fact that (1) the Ark was not the invention of man, but a foreknown, foreordained plan of God; and (2) it was supernaturally revealed to Noah by the word of God (Hebrews 11:7).

We now come to a most interesting detail in the record of Noah's Ark. While Noah had no part in planning the Ark, he nevertheless was given a part in building the physical structure of the Ark. We hope to show you that this was a shadow and a figure of the *Incarnation* of the Lord Jesus of which the Ark was a type. The Ark was designed and planned by God, but it was built by Noah. The instructions were clear:

> Make thee an ark of gopher wood; . . . pitch it within and without with pitch (Genesis 6:14).

The Redeemer of mankind, in order to substitute for man, must Himself be a man. While the Ark was God's divine design, the Ark itself must be built by the sinner who was to be saved from the Flood. The Saviour must be both *God* and *Man*. He must be man to atone for man's sin; He must be God in order to bear the infinite penalty of man's sin. Because He was a man, He could stand in man's place. Because He was God, He could bear in a few hours the eternal, infinite judgment of God upon sin. The spiritually enlightened mind cannot fail to see in this a shadow of the Incarnation — the part that humanity was to play in preparing the Saviour Jesus as the Ark of safety. The Saviour must have a human body and nature as well as divine. Noah was therefore commanded to build the Ark. Millenniums later the One who was foreshadowed by all this came into the world — the product of a human being, called in the Scripture the *Seed of the woman*. The Apostle Paul makes it crystal-clear in Galatians 4:

> But when the fulness of the time was come, God sent forth his Son, *made of a woman*, made under the law,
> To redeem them that were under the law, that we might receive the adoption of sons (Galatians 4:4, 5).

This was the fulfillment of the protevangelium in Genesis 3:15,

> And I will put enmity between thee and the woman, and between thy seed and her seed; it shall bruise thy head, and thou shalt bruise his heel.

Jesus Christ was the eternal Son of God, pre-existent from eternity, but in the fullness of time came into the world as the incarnated Son of God, with a human body and nature prepared by God within the womb of a virgin mother. Yes, God designed it all, but Noah must build the Ark.

PERFECT SAFETY

The typology of the Ark as a figure of Christ is so rich, so wide in its application to our Lord, that we can only select a very few of the details which unmistakably remind us of and point us to Him. The Ark was the safest ship which was ever built. It was completely unsinkable. There could be no storm great or violent enough to cause it to flounder or sink. It was a perfect place of refuge first of all because it was designed by the Lord God Almighty Himself. The security of all those in the Ark was fully guaranteed and this for a number of reasons, all of which are true and typical of Him of whom the Ark was a picture.

1. The Ark was a place of security because the designer and architect Himself was present in the Ark with its occupants. The record speaks volumes as we read in Genesis 7:1,

> And the LORD said unto Noah, *Come* thou and all thy house into the ark; . . .

Notice the word, *come*. Interestingly enough this is the first time the word "come" occurs in our Bible. God did not say to Noah, "Now the Ark is ready, and it is safe, so do not hesitate to go in, for I will be out here watching over you to prevent any harm." This would have been enough for Noah, but this is not what God did. Instead He went into the Ark *first,* and then invited Noah and his family to come and join Him. If the Ark went down, it would carry God down with it. His own presence was the guarantee of the greatest safety.

This reminds me of a conversation I had with a very close friend of mine who has been a chief pilot on one of our great international airlines, flying over the North and South American continents, the seas and the mountains. He has just completed twenty-five years of commercial flying these millions of miles. One day I said to him, "Don't you find the responsibility of carrying more than a hundred passengers in your great jet plane a tremendous strain on you? How does it feel to realize that you are responsible for all those lives behind you?" His answer first stunned me, and then I understood. He said, "I never think of the safety of those passengers. I only think of my own safety." I say, at first I misunderstood, but the truth soon dawned on me. He was not indifferent to the safety of his passengers, but he knew their safety depended on *his own.* The best protection he could give his passengers was to be alert every minute to his job as pilot of the plane. It is a weak illustration, I realize, but it carries the lesson that with God in the Ark, Noah was safe. This was the lesson the disciples of Jesus had not yet learned in the great storm in Matthew 8. They came to the sleeping Jesus, and cried:

Lord, save us: we perish (Matthew 8:25).

They had not yet learned the lesson that when Jesus is in the ship, *it cannot sink.*

2. Notice further the security of the occupants of the Ark, because they had nothing to do with handling the Ark. Evidently the Ark had no sails, no oars, no motor or engine, no rudder, and no pilot house. God Himself directed the course of the great ship. The common idea that the Ark just drifted aimlessly upon the roaring waters is as far from the truth as anything can be. It was carefully piloted and steered

by the hand of Him who said, "Come in." It was being piloted to a safe goal, Mt. Ararat, and a safe landing. So, too, when we trust Christ and come into the Ark of safety, we are not left to drift aimlessly upon the tide, but every moment brings us nearer Heaven and Home.

NOAH'S WORK IN THE ARK

God designed and planned the Ark, and Noah was absolutely secure, but there was plenty for Noah to do. His work was cut out for him. It must have been quite a task to care for and feed all the animals and keep things in order. Now Noah didn't do this to keep from being ejected from the Ark, but because he was safe in the Ark. So, too, the believer in Christ, safe in the "ark of salvation," has a responsibility and duty to care for those who have been entrusted to his care. Paul says in Philippians,

> . . . work out your own salvation with fear and trembling.
> For it is God which worketh in you both to will and to do of his good pleasure (Philippians 2:12, 13).

We are to work *out* what God has already worked *in*. Salvation is God's gift, but we must work to cultivate the fruits of salvation.

3. While the door was open, anyone and all who believed God's word could come in. But once the door was shut, no one else could come in. However, there is one little phrase in the account which is often overlooked. It is the record that when the door was shut, *no one could get out again*. Notice carefully Genesis 7:16,

> And they that went in, went in male and female of all flesh, as God had commanded him: *and the* LORD *shut him in.*

Notice that phrase, for it is inspired, "And the Lord shut him in." God did not say, "Now Noah, shut the door and slide the bar, or snap the lock." Oh, no! The Lord does not place the safety of His own in the hands of men, of preacher or priest. He Himself snaps the lock, and He it is of whom it is said that He

> . . . openeth, and no man shutteth; and shutteth, and no man openeth (Revelation 3:7).

In conclusion, one or two additional observations. There was only *one Ark*. God did not provide a fleet of ships and say, "You may have your choice," but it was the *only* ship available. There are religions without number, but there is only *one way of salvation*. Jesus said,

> I am the door: by me if any man enter in, he shall be saved . . . (John 10:9).

> . . . I am the way, the truth, and the life: no man cometh unto the Father, but by me (John 14:6).

12

COMPLETE ATONEMENT

When we began this series of portraits of Christ in the Book of Genesis, we planned to devote just one chapter to the typology of the Ark of Noah as pointing to the Lord Jesus Christ as our only place of security and safety. However, we had not gone very far until we discovered that we had entered upon a veritable mine of spiritual treasures, and the lessons which progressively opened up before us were inexhaustible. As we dwelt upon one aspect of the typology of the Ark, other truths hitherto not seen jumped up at us, so that even in these four chapters we devote to the Ark as a figure of Christ, we shall only touch the very fringe of the infinite mine of revelation; we shall be able only to dip our toes in the limitless expanse of revelation suggested by the story of the Flood and its great lessons of salvation.

Jesus accepted the record of the Flood and the Ark of Noah as historic fact, and referred to it repeatedly. In answer to the question of His disciples concerning the signs of His coming again, He referred them to the days of Noah, and said:

> But as the days of Noe were, so shall also the coming
> of the Son of man be (Matthew 24:37).

In our previous chapters on the Ark we noted a number of things:

1. It was all designed and planned by God.

2. Man's part was in building the physical structure — a prophecy of the Incarnation of the Saviour by birth of a human mother.

3. The message of salvation through the Ark was supernaturally revealed.

4. It was the only place of refuge. There was only *one* Ark.

Now we are ready to notice some of the other details and their lessons in pointing us to the Lord Jesus our Saviour. Noah was ordered by God to make the Ark three stories high. We read in Genesis 6:16,

> . . . with lower, second, and third stories shalt thou make it.

I must confess that I am not just sure of the correct interpretation and meaning of the three stories of the Ark, but it must have some spiritual meaning or it would not have been mentioned. We can only make a suggestion or two as to its probable meaning. Do we have here a picture of the Trinity as represented by the Ark? We know the Ark is a picture of Jesus Christ, and Christ was God. On earth He represented all the three persons of the Godhead. He said: "I and my Father are one" (John 10:30). When Philip said to Jesus, "Shew us the Father, and it sufficeth us" (John 14:8),

> Jesus saith unto him, Have I been so long time with you, and yet hast thou not known me, Philip? he that hath seen me hath seen the Father; and how sayest thou then, Shew us the Father?
> Believest thou not that I am in the Father, and the Father in me? . . .
> Believe me that I am in the Father, and the Father in me: or else believe me for the very works' sake (John 14:9-11).

Paul tells us that,

> . . . God was in Christ, reconciling the world unto
> himself . . . (II Corinthians 5:19).

Even as the Father dwelt in Christ, so too the blessed
third person of the Trinity, the Holy Spirit, dwelt in the
person of Jesus Christ. At the baptism of Jesus as recorded
by Luke we read:

> . . . it came to pass, that Jesus also being baptized, and
> praying, the heaven was opened,
> And the Holy Ghost descended in a bodily shape like
> a dove upon him, and a voice came from heaven, which
> said, Thou art my beloved Son; in thee I am well pleased
> (Luke 3:21, 22).

Jesus Christ was the incarnate representation of the entire Godhead: Father, Son and Holy Spirit. He was the
embodiment of the Trinity. He was the ambassador for
both the Father and the Holy Spirit here upon the earth.
There are a goodly number of passages in the New Testament which clearly teach that the Triune Godhead dwelt
in the person of Christ (Ephesians 1:23; 3:19; Colossians
1:19). We quote here just one which seems to establish
this truth beyond question:

> For in him [Christ] dwelleth all the fulness of the
> Godhead bodily.
> And ye are complete in him, which is the head of all
> principality and power (Colossians 2:9, 10).

From these Scripture passages we believe that the three
stories of the Ark, which is such a clear type of Christ, may
very well point to the Trinity: Father, Son and Holy Ghost,
all being active in the salvation of Noah and his family.

Another interpretation is presented, which we merely mention, that the three levels of the Ark represent the complete
salvation and provision for those who take refuge in Christ.
It has been suggested that we have here a picture of our

complete, ultimate redemption of *body, soul* and *spirit*. The ground floor of the Ark was for storage of food and provisions for their protracted sojourn in the Ark, and thus, since it provided for the physical need of the occupants, it represents the *body*. The second story, it is intimated, was for the animals, and the place of activity for Noah and his family for caring for their charges. It was the place of work and so represents the *soul* and its spiritual activities and work. The upper story would then represent the dwelling place for Noah and his family for fellowship, rest and communion. This would signify the *spirit*. Whether these interpretations are the correct ones may be questioned by some of our readers, but we throw them out as something to think about. They may not be important, but if they stimulate to further study, then it will still prove profitable.

Only One Window

We cannot leave the study of the Ark of Noah without a few words about its peculiar structure. It seems to have been more of a *scow* than a ship, without rounded bow or pointed prow. From the record we assume it was a flat-bottomed skiff. It had, as we have seen, only one door. It also had only one window described as being a square hole in the flat roof about eighteen by eighteen inches. It was covered by a window or hatch. The spiritual application of all this is clear. Noah and his family were not to be looking *out* upon the raging waves and pounding billows with its scene of destruction about and beneath them, but *up* only to Heaven. This is the lesson God would have His people to learn. The same lesson is suggested by Israel's journey for forty years through a howling, barren wilderness. He furnished them also with a window above, in the form of a pillar of cloud by day and a glowing pillar of fire by night. This cloud was not only for the purpose of guiding them on their way, but very evidently also to remind them to *look up,* and not to be overwhelmed by the difficulties and trials of the wilderness.

PLACE OF REST

One detail often overlooked in the study of the Ark as a portrait of Christ is the provision the Lord made in the Ark for rest and relaxation. A little phrase is inserted in verse 14:

> . . . rooms shalt thou make in the ark . . . (Genesis 6:14).

The Hebrew word translated "rooms" in this verse is *kane* and means literally "a nest." God not only provided for the safety of the occupants of the Ark, but He made provision for their comfort as well. Noah was told to make "nests" in the Ark. Our Lord Jesus of whom all this is a type, said many years later:

> In my Father's house are many mansions [dwelling places]: . . . I go to prepare a place for you (John 14:2).

ABSOLUTE SECURITY

Before concluding this chapter we must call your attention once more to the picture of absolute security and safety which God provided for those who had entered the Ark. In order for the Ark to be a place of absolute safety it must be absolutely waterproof. This was provided for in a number of ways. First, there was only one door and that door was locked by God Himself. There was only one window, and that on the roof and only eighteen inches square. But the Lord made an additional provision for keeping out the waters of judgment. The Ark itself was made of cypress, in itself an excellent wood for exposure to water, and was completely sealed both inside and outside by a waterproofing material common in that area. We read in Genesis 6,

> Make thee an ark of gopher wood; . . . pitch it within and without with pitch (Genesis 6:14).

The Hebrew word here translated as "pitch" is not the usual word used elsewhere which is *zepheth* and simply means a bituminous substance such as asphalt. The material Noah used for the covering of the Ark may have been the same material, but an entirely different word is used. The word translated "pitch" in Genesis 6 is the word *kaphar* (verb) or *kopher* (noun). It is the only place this word is so translated, although it is used seventy times elsewhere in the Bible. And now be ready for a real revelation. The word *kaphar,* translated "pitch" in the building of the Ark and used seventy times elsewhere, is in every other occurrence translated "atonement." The word itself simply means "a covering," but is translated "atonement" in every other place. Literally, therefore, we might read Genesis 6:14, "Thou shalt 'cover' it within and without with *atonement.*"

We have already seen that the only atonement God would receive for sin was a blood sacrifice. After Adam's fig leaves had proven inadequate, the Lord came and slew a substitutionary animal and covered Adam and Eve with the bloody skins. Here already in Paradise God revealed that the only adequate covering for sin is *blood,* and that only *blood* can make an atonement for the *soul.* We saw it again in the experience of Cain and Abel, for Cain's sacrifice was rejected because he ignored the blood, while Abel's was accepted because he brought a bleeding lamb. This is God's rule throughout the entire Scriptures that "without shedding of blood [there] is no remission" (Hebrews 9:22).

After Israel had left Egypt under the sheltering blood of the Passover Lamb, one of the first things they were to learn was the sanctity and importance of the blood. Again and again God reminds them of the cardinal principle, "no atonement without blood." Noah had scarcely left the Ark when God gave the command about the blood. As soon as Noah left the Ark he builded an altar and presented the blood to the Lord.

> And Noah builded an altar unto the LORD; and took of every clean beast, and of every clean fowl, and offered burnt offerings on the altar (Genesis 8:20).

It was right after this that God gave the command concerning the sacredness of the blood, when he said in Genesis 9:4,

> But flesh with the life thereof, which is the blood thereof, shall ye not eat.

This prohibition was repeated. In Leviticus 7:26 God said,

> Moreover ye shall eat no manner of blood, whether it be of fowl or of beast, . . .

The reason was because blood speaks of atonement and the covering for sin, and it is not to be despised. This is made clear in Leviticus 17,

> And whatsoever man there be of the house of Israel, or of the strangers that sojourn among you, that eateth any manner of blood; I will even set my face against that soul that eateth blood, and will cut him off from among his people (Leviticus 17:10).

AND WHY?

> For the life of the flesh is in the blood: and I have given it to you upon the altar to make an *atonement* for your souls . . . (Leviticus 17:11).

Do you realize that the word "atonement" in this verse is a translation of the same word translated "pitch" in Genesis 6, the pitch with which the Ark was covered within and without? Do you know that when the High Priest went into the Holy of Holies (Leviticus 16) and sprinkled the blood upon the mercy seat over the broken law, that he made *atonement* for their sins and the same word translated "pitch" in Genesis 6, is used?

The Ark was symbolically covered inside and outside with the "blood of atonement." No wonder there were no casualties in the Ark. Everyone that went in was kept, and came out safely. The Holy Spirit evidently wanted us to know how secure the occupants of the Ark were, for He records:

And Noah went forth, and his sons, and his wife, and his sons' wives with him:

Every beast, *every* creeping thing, and *every* fowl, and whatsoever creepeth upon the earth, after their kinds, *went forth out of the ark* (Genesis 8:18, 19).

Not a single one was missing, for the Ark foreshadowed the One who millenniums later said to His disciples,

My sheep hear my voice, and I know them, and they follow me:

And I give unto them eternal life; and they shall never perish, neither shall any man pluck them out of my hand.

My Father, which gave them me, is greater than all; and no man is able to pluck them out of my Father's hand (John 10:27-29).

Oh, sinner, hear once more God's invitation to Noah:

. . . Come thou and all thy house into the ark . . . (Genesis 7:1).

13

DELIVERED IN JOY

The word "type" does not occur anywhere in our English Bible. Neither does the word "typology" appear and yet the study of types in the Old Testament is one of the most interesting and rewarding exercises. The word "type" in the original Greek is *tupos* and is translated "figure" or "shadow." Hence we speak of types as figures or shadows of objects or occurrences. A type is an incident or occurrence that is historically true but points to another person, incident, or occurrence in the future. It is a shadow of something to come. We usually cannot identify the object that casts the shadow by the shadow alone, but when the object to whom the figure points is seen, all becomes clear. For instance, we know that Adam was a type of Christ when he was put to sleep and from his wounded side the Lord God builded for him a woman to be an helpmeet for him. Of course, without the record of the New Testament we could never have known the meaning of that first surgical operation performed in the Garden of Eden. But in the light of the New Testament, we see Christ as the Second Man and the last Adam. In the same way we see Calvary plainly in the sacrifice of the first animal when God made coats of skins and covered our first parents.

NOAH'S ARK

In the same way no spiritually enlightened child of God can fail to see in the Ark of Noah God's picture of our Saviour from judgment. Every detail points to some aspect of the work of Christ. In our former chapters on the Ark of Noah as a figure of Christ, we have seen the Ark as an unmistakable figure of our coming Redeemer. The Ark represents the refuge for sinners from the coming judgment. But this does not entirely exhaust the typology. Sometimes, yea, oftentimes, we see a double typology; that is, an incident may be a type or a figure of two different things. Such was the case with Adam. He certainly is a figure and type of the lost sinner in need of salvation. But at the same time he is also a type of the last Adam and the Second Man, Jesus Christ. Such, too, was the case with Isaac, the son of Abraham. As we shall see in the coming chapters, he was a clear type and picture of the Son who was to be sacrificed, but at the same time he was a picture of the sinner who himself needed a Saviour and, therefore, God provided for him a substitute in the ram caught in the bushes (Genesis 22:13).

SAME TRUE OF FLOOD

The Ark was truly a type of Christ as Saviour from coming judgment, but the Flood is also a picture of the Great Tribulation of the end-time, and God's provision for an elect remnant to be brought through the Great Tribulation by Jesus Christ, their Ark of safety. We would remind you again of Jesus' answer to the question of the disciples:

> . . . Tell us, when shall these things be? and what shall be the sign of thy coming, and of the end of the world [age]? (Matthew 24:3).

To this direct and unmistakable question, Jesus answers:

> But as the days of Noe were, so shall also the coming of the Son of man be.

> For as in the days that were *before* the flood . . .
> . . . so shall also the coming of the Son of man be
> (Matthew 24:37-39).

We would call your attention to one word in this passage —
the word *before.* Jesus speaks of conditions *before* the Flood
came. There were only three classes of people on the earth
in the days *before* the Flood, represented by Enoch, Noah
and his family, and the wicked who were destroyed in the
judgment of the Flood. Enoch was translated before the
floods came; Noah and his family were carried safely through
the Flood; and the wicked perished in the Flood. The same
three classes of people are in the world today, and will be
at the coming of the Son of Man. Paul identifies the only
three kinds of people living today in I Corinthians 10:32,

> Give none offence, neither to the Jews, nor to the
> Gentiles, nor to the church of God.

Every individual belongs to one of these three groups. A
Jew is a physical descendant of Abraham through Isaac and
Jacob. Israelites are descendants of Israel. All who are not
Israelites or Jews are classified as Gentiles. But there is a
third group, consisting of both Jews and Gentiles, and called
the Church of the living God, the Body of Christ. Every-
one who has believed in Jesus as the Son of God, and trusted
Him for salvation is a member of the one true Church, the
Body of Christ. With these three groups of people in mind,
think again about the words of Jesus:

> For as in the days that were *before* the flood . . .
> . . . so shall also the coming of the Son of man be
> (Matthew 24:38, 39).

As it was in Noah's day, so shall it be just prior to the
Second Coming of Christ. In the days before the Flood, we
have the record of Enoch who was translated *before* the
Flood. There was a second company (Noah and his family)
who passed safely *through* the Flood, and then the third
group who perished *in* the Flood. This is to be repeated, for
the Lord has promised that before He visits the world in

judgment in the coming Great Tribulation, He will call out all true believers. Paul speaks of this in many places, but we refer you to the classic passage:

> For the Lord himself shall descend from heaven with a shout, with the voice of the archangel, and with the trump of God: and the dead in Christ shall rise first:
>
> Then we which are alive and remain shall be caught up together with them in the clouds, to meet the Lord in the air: and so shall we ever be with the Lord (I Thessalonians 4:16, 17).

Then the Day of the Lord will be ushered in, and the days of earth's greatest tribulation be experienced, a time so terrible that except those days were shortened, there should no flesh be saved. But while the Church is raptured, Israel is still here, and God has made provision for the faithful remnant of Jacob's seed, that they will not be destroyed by the wrath of the false Messiah, the Antichrist. Just as Enoch was translated before the judgment fell, and Noah was made safe in the Ark, so also, after the Church has been raptured and the Tribulation days begin, He will prepare a place of safety for the believing remnant of Israel. Soon after the Rapture of the Church, the greatest revival in history will sweep over the nation of Israel, and thousands upon thousands of the Jews will acknowledge Jesus Christ as their Messiah. They will become the special target for the Antichrist, but God will protect them, even as Noah was protected in the Ark. Just as the exact number of souls saved in the Ark is recorded, so the exact number of the saved of Israel is recorded. There were exactly eight saved in the Ark. There will be exactly 144,000 Israelites saved in the Tribulation, and supernaturally preserved through that awful day.

THE SEAL OF GOD

All of this had already been predicted and promised by the prophets in many passages. Ezekiel says concerning Israel:

> For I will take you from among the heathen [Gentiles], and gather you out of all countries, and will bring you into your own land.
>
> Then will I sprinkle clean water upon you, and ye shall be clean . . .
>
> And ye shall dwell in the land that I gave to your fathers; and ye shall be my people, and I will be your God (Ezekiel 36:24, 25, 28).

Or, listen carefully to the prophet Jeremiah in speaking about that great and terrible day of earth's greatest tribulation when the nation of Israel will be persecuted in a measure never before experienced in history:

> Alas! for that day is great, so that none is like it: it is even the *time of Jacob's trouble, but he shall be saved out of it.*
>
> Therefore fear thou not, O my servant Jacob, saith the Lord; neither be dismayed, O Israel: for, lo, I will save thee from afar, and thy seed from the land of their captivity; and Jacob shall return, and shall be in rest, and be quiet, and none shall make him afraid.
>
> For I am with thee, saith the Lord, to save thee: though I make a full end of all nations whither I have scattered thee, yet will I not make a full end of thee: but I will correct thee in measure, and will not leave thee altogether unpunished (Jeremiah 30:7, 10, 11).

After the Church is translated, there will be a remnant of the true Israel converted and they will become the greatest missionaries of all time, with the result that a great revival will break out and a multitude from every people, tongue, tribe and nation will be converted. They with Israel shall suffer great persecution, but they will be delivered by the personal return of Jesus Christ with His Church. John says in Revelation 7, concerning the remnant of Israel during the Tribulation:

> . . . Hurt not the earth, neither the sea, nor the trees, till we have sealed the servants of our God in their foreheads.
>
> And I heard the number of them which were sealed:

and there were sealed an hundred and forty and four
thousand of all the tribes of the children of Israel.
Of the tribe of Juda were sealed twelve thousand. Of
the tribe of Reuben were sealed twelve thousand . . .
(Revelation 7:3-5).

John continues naming all of the twelve tribes individually.
This will be a nation born in a day. One hundred and forty-
four thousand converted Israelites, supernaturally protected
by God and sealed against death, will go forth during those
awful days of the Tribulation, preaching the Gospel of the
Kingdom, resulting in the greatest revival of all time. Immediately after the record of the sealing of the 144,000 Jews,
John continues under inspiration:

After this I beheld, and, lo, a great multitude, which
no man could number, of all nations, and kindreds, and
people, and tongues, stood before the throne, and before the Lamb, clothed with white robes, and palms in
their hands;
And cried with a loud voice, saying, Salvation to our
God which sitteth upon the throne, and unto the Lamb
(Revelation 7:9, 10).

This great multitude consists of Tribulation believers, pre-
sumably converted by the testimony of the 144,000. This is
made very clear, for one of the elders explains to John:

. . . These are they which came out of [the] great
tribulation, and have washed their robes, and made
them white in the blood of the Lamb (Revelation 7:14).

ORDER OF EVENTS

This Tribulation period of seven years will be suddenly
ended by the personal return of the Lord Jesus to deliver
His people and judge the wicked nations. So remember the
three groups of people before the Flood: Enoch representing
those who will be raptured *before* the Tribulation; then
Noah and his family representing the faithful remnant of
Israel who will pass through the Tribulation to emerge upon a
renewed and cleaned earth. This leaves the third group, the

wicked nations who will perish in the judgment of those days.

As we conclude these few chapters on the typology of the Ark we realize that we have merely skimmed the surface, we have scarcely moistened our feet in the edge of God's infinite ocean of revelation. If we have stimulated you to dig deeper into this great type of the work of Christ, we shall feel we are well repaid. If these studies have created a hunger for more of Christ in the Word, then the many hours and days of study, research, and prayer will not have been in vain. As we wrote this book, the words of the wise man of Ecclesiastes came frequently to mind:

> And further, by these, my son, be admonished: of making many books there is no end; and much study is a weariness of the flesh (Ecclesiastes 12:12).

I have found it so, and sometimes I wondered if it was worthwhile to write another book, but when I considered the fruit of my own study, and the blessing I received from digging into the bottomless mine of God's precious truth, I was constrained to put it in writing that others (I hope) might share somewhat in the blessing of finding "things old and new" in this inexhaustible storehouse of truth. We are deeply conscious of the many other lessons this story of the Flood and the Ark contains, which we have passed over. We do hope our readers will be prompted to study for themselves this great picture of Christ and His redemptive program. The most pressing question we would ask as we close our series on the Ark is this: "Have you taken refuge in the Ark of God's provision?" The people in Noah's day could enter only while the door was open. Once it was shut by God, it was forever too late. The door of salvation is still open to you. It may be shut before the day is over. Why not heed the call:

> Come unto me, all ye that labour and are heavy laden, and I will give you rest (Matthew 11:28).

14

SON OF PROMISE

The Book of Genesis contains fifty chapters, and is the book of beginnings. Science may continue its search for the beginning of things, but it will never find a better answer than the opening verse of the Bible, "In the beginning God created the heaven and the earth" (Genesis 1:1). Of the fifty chapters in Genesis, the first eleven chapters cover a span of almost two thousand years, while the last thirty-nine chapters cover a period of less than four hundred years. Only eleven chapters to tell us what happened the first two thousand years on earth — thirty-nine chapters to tell us what happened in the comparatively brief four hundred years following. The first eleven chapters cover the record of creation, the fall, the coming of the Flood, the building of the Tower of Babel, and give the brief history of a large number of individuals. However, soon after the Flood, man again forgot God and drifted into idolatry. Before the knowledge of the Lord should disappear from the earth completely, God stepped in, and called a man by the name of Abram (later called Abraham), and in sovereign grace separated him from his idolatrous family in Ur of the Chaldees. This was to be a new beginning, in order to carry out God's plan of redemption through His Son, Jesus Christ. Abram's history begins in the closing verses of Genesis 11, and then in Genesis 12 we read:

111

Now the Lord had said unto Abram, Get thee out of
thy country, and from thy kindred, and from thy father's
house, unto a land that I will shew thee (Genesis 12:1).

God was now to abandon the nations, and begin to deal
with one particular nation, the descendants of Abram through
Isaac and Jacob. The entire balance of the Book of Genesis
(chapters 12 to 50) is therefore occupied with four men:
Abraham, Isaac, Jacob and Joseph. Believing as we do in
the divine purpose, pattern, and inspiration of the Scriptures, there must be a reason for the emphasis on the history
of just these four men. We believe we have the answer in
the purpose for which the book was written. The Bible is
the Book of *redemption.* While it is scientifically infallible
it is not primarily a Book of science. While it is geographi-
cally accurate, it is not a world atlas. While it predicts the
international and political fortunes of the nations, it is not
primarily a Book on political science. All these matters are
secondary to the one purpose of the Book: to reveal the plan
of redemption through the Redeemer, the Lord Jesus Christ.
It began in the promise of the seed of the woman, was elab-
orated in the slaying of an animal to provide coats of skins,
and was illustrated in God's provision of an Ark of salvation.

THE LIGHT BRIGHTENS

When we come to this new section of the Book, beginning
with the history of Abraham, the typology and purpose of
the Book of Genesis becomes more clear. In the history of
these four men, Abraham, Isaac, Jacob and Joseph, we have
the four great steps in the redemptive plan. Abraham is the
example of *sovereign election and predestination.* He lived
with his family in Ur of the Chaldees and was a member of
an idol-worshiping family (see Joshua 24:2). There were
other members in this nation and in this family, who probably were no worse than Abraham, but God picked him out
from among all the rest, and separated him unto Himself.

Just as Abraham illustrates God's sovereign election, so

Isaac is the example of God's *sovereign grace* in calling him. He was the youngest of Abraham's children. Ishmael was the elder of the two and Abraham had chosen Ishmael to be the heir, but God said, No,

> . . . in Isaac shall thy seed be called (Genesis 21:12).

When we come to Jacob we find a most striking illustration of *justification by faith through grace.* Again, Jacob was the younger of the twins, and legally the birthright should have gone to Esau. But Jacob, by conniving and scheming with his mother, deprived Esau of his portion and deceived his blind father, was driven into a far country where he, by scheming and clever dealing, almost ruined his Uncle Laban. Jacob was a crook, a deceiver, a supplanter, a rascal. By comparison, Esau was a gentleman, but grace turns nature upside down, and God in sovereign grace chose Jacob and said, "The elder shall serve the younger" (Genesis 25: 23); and again, "Jacob have I loved, but Esau have I hated" (Romans 9:13). Jacob then is the example of *justification by faith without works.*

Now we come to Joseph who represents our *glorification.* Sold by his brethren, he was exalted to the throne of Egypt. In Abraham, Isaac, Jacob, and Joseph, we see the four steps of our redemption:

1. Sovereign predestination.
2. Effective calling.
3. Justification by faith.
4. Glorification by grace.

I am quite sure the Apostle Paul must have had this in mind when he wrote in Romans 8,

> For whom he did foreknow, he also did *predestinate* to be conformed to the image of his Son, that he might be the firstborn among many brethren.
> Moreover whom he did predestinate, them he also *called*: and whom he called, them he also *justified*: and whom he justified, them he also *glorified* (Romans 8: 29, 30).

Isaac, Type of Christ

In this series of messages we have been especially occupied with the various types, shadows, and figures of the Lord Jesus in the Book of Genesis. As we move along the types and shadows become more clear, and when we come to the story of Isaac we have such a clear picture of the coming Son of Promise that one scarcely knows where to begin. Isaac, the son of Abraham, is a clear and unmistakable picture of the Lord Jesus Christ in His *miraculous conception* and *virgin birth*, in His *willing obedience* to the Father, in His *sacrifice* upon the altar, and in His *Resurrection*. We shall take them up in their order. The Apostle Paul says in Galatians that the Gospel was preached before unto Abraham, and we shall have no difficulty finding the Gospel in the story of the birth, the death, and the Resurrection of Jesus Christ, as pictured in Isaac.

A Son of Promise

The first thing we would have you notice about Isaac was that he was promised long before he was born. When Abraham left his native land, the Lord promised him a seed (Genesis 12:3). But even though long delayed, God kept His promise. Over twenty-five years dragged by between the promise of a seed and the birth of Isaac. God made promise of the seed of the woman in Genesis 3:15, and almost four thousand years went by before it was fulfilled. Notice further that the birth of Isaac was exactly at the appointed time. Of his birth we read:

> And the Lord visited Sarah as he had said, and the Lord did unto Sarah as he had spoken.
>
> For Sarah conceived, and bare Abraham a son in his old age, at the set time of which God had spoken to him (Genesis 21:1, 2).

In all this he is a perfect type of the Lord Jesus Christ. He too was promised many years before, and His birth seemed to be long delayed, but when the time came which God had promised, the seed was born. Jesus too was born in the fullness of time, born of a woman, and made under the law (Galatians 4:4).

THE STRIKING PARALLEL

The whole story of the birth of Isaac bears such a striking parallel to the birth of Jesus Christ that we call your attention to a number of similar situations which cannot be overlooked:

1. The birth of Isaac was by a supernatural conception, and his birth involved a miracle. Of this we shall have more to say later.

2. The birth of Isaac was foretold long before the time of his birth, and his name was announced before he was born. The Lord said to Abraham when He gave promise of the son:

> . . . and thou shalt call his name Isaac: and I will establish my covenant with him for an everlasting covenant . . . (Genesis 17:19).

The name of Jesus, the antitype of Isaac, was also announced beforehand. We read in Matthew 1, concerning Joseph, the husband of Mary, while debating what to do with Mary his wife after he found that she was with child:

> But while he thought on these things, behold, the angel of the Lord appeared unto him in a dream, saying, Joseph, thou son of David, fear not to take unto thee Mary thy wife: for that which is conceived in her is of the Holy Ghost.
>
> And she shall bring forth a son, and thou shalt call his name JESUS: for he shall save his people from their sins (Matthew 1:20, 21).

3. Abraham was confused when God promised him a son in his old age, by his senile wife, Sarah. We read in Genesis 17:

> And God said unto Abraham, As for Sarai thy wife,
> thou shalt not call her name Sarai, but Sarah shall her
> name be.
> And I will . . . give thee a son also of her . . .
> Then Abraham fell upon his face, and laughed, and
> said in his heart, Shall . . . Sarah, that is ninety years
> old, bear? (Genesis 17:15-17).

When Joseph found Mary to be with child, he was equally
confused and being the just man that he was he sought to
protect Mary from shame and to put her away privately.
Matthew tells us:

> Then Joseph her husband, being a just man, and not
> willing to make her a publick example, was minded to
> put her away privily.
> But while he thought on these things, behold, the
> angel of the Lord appeared unto him in a dream, saying,
> Joseph, thou son of David, fear not to take unto thee
> Mary thy wife: for that which is conceived in her is of
> the Holy Ghost (Matthew 1:19, 20).

4. The same parallel exists between the reaction of Sarah
and Mary before the supernaturally conceived children were
born. When the Lord came to Abraham and promised him
a son by his ninety-year-old Sarah, it completely confused
her and she considered it utterly impossible. The record is
plain:

> And he [God] said, I will certainly return unto thee
> according to the time of life; and, lo, Sarah thy wife
> shall have a son. And Sarah heard it in the tent door,
> which was behind him.
> Therefore Sarah laughed within herself, saying, After
> I am waxed old shall I have pleasure, my lord being old
> also? (Genesis 18:10, 12).

She just could not understand it, and it confused her, but
the Lord came to her with the answer:

> And the LORD said to Abraham, Wherefore did Sarah
> laugh, saying, Shall I of a surety bear a child, which am
> old?

> *Is any thing too hard for the* LORD? At the time appointed I will return unto thee, according to the time of life, and Sarah *shall have a son* (Genesis 18:13, 14).

One cannot fail to see the very same reaction, and God's answer to Mary when she was confused about her own unexplainable condition. An angel from Heaven came to Mary just as the celestial visitors had come to Abraham's tent, and

> . . . the angel said unto her, Fear not, Mary: for thou hast found favour with God.
>
> And, behold, thou shalt conceive in thy womb, and bring forth a son, and shalt call his name JESUS (Luke 1:30, 31).

This left Mary in a state of utter confusion and so she asks essentially the same question Sarah asked:

> . . . How shall this be, seeing I know not a man?
>
> And the angel answered and said unto her, The Holy Ghost shall come upon thee, and the power of the Highest shall overshadow thee; therefore also that holy thing which shall be born of thee shall be called the Son of God (Luke 1:34, 35).

Before leaving this feature, we must call your attention to one verse in Luke 1:37, "For with God nothing shall be impossible." This was spoken on the occasion of the announcement of the angel concerning the birth of John the Baptist. Elizabeth, the cousin of Mary, was barren, but God performed a miracle, a supernatural conception, and gave her a son by the name of John, and then the angel adds, "For with God nothing shall be impossible" (Luke 1:37).

It is identical in meaning with God's words when announcing the miraculous birth of Isaac when he says in Genesis 18:14, "Is any thing too hard for the LORD?"

Surely this will make a good verse with which to close this chapter. We have seen only a few of the striking details of the birth of Isaac as a type and figure of the birth of the Lord Jesus Christ. In our next chapter we shall show that the supernatural conception of Isaac was just as great a miracle as the Virgin Birth of Christ. The same is true of the birth of John the Baptist. To those who deny the Virgin Birth and the record of the miracles in the Book of Genesis, we would merely ask the question in Genesis 18:14, "Is any thing too hard for the LORD?" and answer it with the words of the angel in Luke 1:37, "For with God nothing shall be impossible."

Applied to the plan of redemption, the answer is the same. The greatest sinner can be saved simply by turning to the Christ of God, believing that with Him nothing is impossible.

15

A MIRACULOUS BIRTH

Do you know that the birth of Isaac, the son of Abraham and Sarah, was a wonderful miracle? Do you know that the birth of John the Baptist was also the result of a supernatural act of God? Isaac, the son of Abraham, is one of the clearest types of the Lord Jesus Christ in the entire Old Testament. Usually he is seen as a type of the Lord Jesus Christ as he was taken to Mt. Moriah and placed there upon the altar of sacrifice by his father Abraham. This certainly was the most dramatic incident in the typology of Isaac as a figure of Christ dying on the cross, but it by no means exhausts the figure of Isaac as a shadow of Christ. Paul in Galatians tells us that the Gospel was preached to Abraham (Galatians 3:8). This Gospel which God revealed to Abraham included not only the sacrificial death of the promised Son, but also His supernatural conception and Virgin Birth as well as His Resurrection and His Second Coming.

THE VIRGIN BIRTH

In this chapter we want to be occupied with the supernatural conception and miraculous birth of Isaac as an outstanding type of Jesus Christ and the absolute faith in the Virgin Birth in order to be saved. No one can be saved who denies the Virgin Birth of Christ, for without the Virgin Birth Jesus was just a man and could not be deity. And if

Jesus be not God, He could not atone for the infinite guilt of sin of mankind, or bear the eternal punishment of hell for sinners. The Virgin Birth is as essential a doctrine as the substitutionary death and bodily Resurrection of Jesus. No wonder Satan's attack is leveled against this particular doctrine. We have already seen in a faint outline the prophecy of this Virgin Birth in the first promise of the Redeemer, when He is called the *seed of the woman,* and not the seed of the *man.* However, when we come to the birth of Isaac, the portrait of Jesus becomes crystal clear. Among the portraits of Jesus in the figures in the Old Testament, none is more clearly and easily recognizable than the man Isaac, with the possible exception of Joseph, and the institution of the Passover in Exodus.

Abraham and Sarah

When Abraham was still in his prime, the Lord called him out of Ur of the Chaldees to migrate to the land of Canaan. God promised the land for a possession, and a seed in whom all the families of the earth would be blessed. On the way from Ur of the Chaldees to Canaan he stopped at Haran, and tarried there for an indefinite time. When Abraham finally left Haran to go to Canaan, he was seventy-five years old (Genesis 12:4). How old he was when he left his homeland we cannot tell, for we do not know how long he tarried in Haran, where he left his father. Finally he arrived in the Promised Land and became exceedingly prosperous. A quarrel erupted between him and his nephew Lot concerning grazing lands, and it was then that God once more repeated His promise of a seed to Abraham. The promise was clear. God said:

> For all the land which thou seest, to thee will I give it, and to thy seed for ever.
> And I will make thy seed as the dust of the earth . . .
> (Genesis 13:15, 16).

But the years dragged wearily on and on, and still there was no sign of the fulfillment of God's promise that He would give a son to Abraham and Sarah. Finally they both became old. Abraham recognized this, and complained rather bitterly to the Lord for His apparent failure to keep His word. Abraham was now one hundred years old and Sarah was ninety. And then God came to them and repeated the promise of a son. Now it became a matter of faith, and God put Abraham to the test to see whether he would trust the Lord to do the impossible. We must remember that at this time both Abraham and Sarah had long ago passed the age of parenthood. The Bible leaves no doubt in this matter. Notice the following passages:

> Now Sarai Abram's wife bare him no children; and she had an handmaid, an Egyptian, whose name was Hagar.
> And Sarai said unto Abram, Behold now, the LORD hath restrained me from bearing: I pray thee, go in unto my maid; it may be that I may obtain children by her. And Abram hearkened to the voice of Sarai (Genesis 16:1, 2).

We mention this here to show that although Abraham believed God and was called the father of the faithful, he also had lapses of faith. There were times in his life when serious doubts and questions arose in his mind. It was in one of these depressed states that the enemy found occasion to tempt him, and as a result, Ishmael, the "son of doubt," was born to trouble Abraham and his descendants ever after. When Ishmael was born Abraham was about eighty-seven years old. Another thirteen years passed by, and in this period of time Abraham became an impotent old man. Sarah already was barren, and now Abraham became impotent. But still the promise of God was unfulfilled. If He was to fulfill this promise, it could only be by a miracle of God to rejuvenate a senile old couple so they could become parents.

The need for a supernatural miracle is emphasized over and
over again. In Genesis 18 we read,

> Now Abraham and Sarah were old and well stricken
> in age; and it [had] ceased to be with Sarah after the
> manner of women (Genesis 18:11).

We can hardly blame Sarah for laughing at the promise
of verse 10,

> . . . I will certainly return unto thee according to the
> time of life; and, lo, Sarah thy wife shall have a son . . .
> (Genesis 18:10).

Yes, indeed, God was about to perform a great miracle,
the first step in the typical Gospel which was to be preached
to Abraham. All this is abundantly confirmed in the New
Testament. The Apostle Paul in commenting on the justification of Abraham by faith asks the question:

> What shall we say then that Abraham our father, as
> pertaining to the flesh, hath found?
> For if Abraham were justified by works, he hath
> whereof to glory; but not before God.
> For what saith the scripture? Abraham believed God,
> and it was counted unto him for righteousness (Romans
> 4:1-3).

Abraham *believed God!* What did he believe? It does
not say he believed in God, but *he believed God.* He believed God's promise of a long-delayed, supernaturally born
son, the type of God's greater Son, the Lord Jesus Christ.
This is clear from Genesis 15, from which Paul quotes. After
Abraham had complained to God for His apparent failure
to give him the son He had promised, God repeated the
promise, and said concerning Eliezer, Abraham's servant:

> . . . This shall not be thine heir; but he that shall come
> forth out of thine own bowels shall be thine heir.
> And he brought him forth abroad, and said, Look now
> toward heaven, and tell the stars, if thou be able to
> number them: and he said unto him, *so shall thy seed
> be* (Genesis 15:4, 5).

Now remember this was when Abraham was one hundred years old, and Sarah was ninety years, and the record plainly says:

> Now Abraham and Sarah were old and well stricken in age; and it ceased to be with Sarah after the manner of women (Genesis 18:11).

It would therefore take a miracle, a supernatural act of God, and Abraham accepted God's promise and we read:

> And he [Abraham] believed in the LORD; and he counted it to him for righteousness (Genesis 15:6).

This is the verse which Paul quotes in Romans 4:3 to illustrate *justification by faith*. How was Abraham justified in the sight of God? By believing God's promise concerning a long-delayed, supernaturally conceived son. God's plan of salvation has not changed today. Following Abraham's example, we too can only be saved by *believing what God says* concerning His supernaturally conceived, virgin-born Son, Jesus Christ.

Commenting on this faith of Abraham, Paul says in Romans 4:

> Who against hope believed in hope, that he might become the father of many nations; according to that which was spoken, So shall thy seed be.
> And being not weak in faith, he [Abraham] considered not his own body now dead, when he was about an hundred years old, neither yet the deadness of Sarah's womb (Romans 4:18, 19).

This passage says Abraham believed *in hope against hope*; human reason gave no basis for hope. According to nature it was against hope, but yet it says he believed *in hope*. This hope was founded on the word of God, and not on reason or logic. This will explain the expression, "who against hope believed in hope." The next verse (Romans 4:19) can best be rendered:

> "And being not weak in faith, he gave no considera-
> tion to the fact that he was physically impotent and
> Sarah's womb was dead."

He realized that it was contrary to nature, but he believed
it because God said it, and so:

> He staggered not at the promise of God through un-
> belief; but was strong in faith, giving glory to God;
> And being fully persuaded that, what he had prom-
> ised, he was able also to perform.
> And therefore it was imputed to him for righteous-
> ness (Romans 4:20-22).

Abraham believed what God said about his son, just because God said it, and for no other reason. He believed in
the same way that we are to believe in the Virgin Birth of
Christ. And Sarah, the wife of Abraham, shared this vic-
torious faith. We read in Hebrews 11:

> Through faith also Sara herself received strength to
> conceive seed, and was delivered of a child when she
> was past age, because she judged him faithful who had
> promised.
> Therefore sprang there even of one, and *him as good
> as dead,* so many as the stars of the sky in multitude . . .
> (Hebrews 11:11, 12).

Isaac then, as a type of Christ, is first and foremost a figure,
a shadow, and a prophecy of the Virgin Birth of the Lord
Jesus Christ. Without faith in the Virgin Birth there can be
no faith in His atoning death and Resurrection. God's plan
of salvation has not changed. To the question, "How are
we justified in God's sight?" — Paul says, "What saith the
Scripture? Abraham believed God and it was counted to
him for righteousness." He believed God's Word concerning the Son.

It is the only way of salvation. After showing how Abraham was justified by faith in Romans 4, he continues:

> Now it (the record of Abraham's faith) was not writ-
> ten for his sake alone, that it was imputed to him;

But for us also, to whom it shall be imputed, if we believe on him that raised up Jesus our Lord from the dead;

Who was delivered for our offences, and was raised again for our justification (Romans 4:23-25).

So we repeat again, and shall repeat again and again, that salvation is believing what God has to say concerning His Son Jesus Christ. All Abraham had was the promise of God. It was contrary to reason and nature, but he believed what God said. In I John 5 we read:

If we receive the witness of men, the witness of God is greater: for this is the witness of God which he hath testified of his Son.

He that believeth on the Son of God hath the witness in himself: he that believeth not God hath made him a liar; because he believeth not the *record* that God gave of his Son.

And this is the record, that God hath given to us eternal life, and this life is in his Son (I John 5:9-11).

To be saved one must accept by faith the record which God has given us concerning His Son Jesus Christ. The only place where you can find this record is in the Bible, the Word of God. And this Word says:

Whosoever believeth that Jesus is the Christ is born of God . . . (I John 5:1).

For God so loved the world, that he gave his only begotten Son, that whosoever believeth in him should not perish, but have everlasting life (John 3:16).

16

IN GOD'S OWN TIME

The birth of Isaac, the son of Abraham, was a miracle, for Isaac was born when Abraham was totally impotent at the age of one hundred, and Sarah was completely barren at the age of ninety. But God had promised to Abraham and Sarah a son, and a seed which would become the blessing of the whole world. Even after the time had passed where, in the natural course of events, Abraham and Sarah could become parents of a child, the Lord reassured them. In Genesis 18:11 we are told that both Abraham and Sarah were old and senile and Sarah laughed at the promise of a son. Then God replies:

> Is any thing too hard for the LORD? At the time appointed I will return unto thee, according to the time of life, and Sarah shall have a son (Genesis 18:14).

And so it was. When God had performed the miracle of rejuvenation on Abraham and Sarah, He fulfilled His promise. It was not too hard for the Lord. The record is refreshing and encouraging.

> And the LORD visited Sarah *as he had said*, and the LORD did unto Sarah *as he had spoken*.
> For Sarah conceived, and bare Abraham a son in his old age, at the *set time* of which God had spoken to him (Genesis 21:1, 2).

We call your especial attention to two phrases in these verses. They are, *as he had said,* and *as he had spoken.* God kept His word, and that is the great lesson hidden here but usually overlooked. God did as He had promised, even though it was long delayed, and apparently impossible. But God "visited Sarah as he had said, and did unto her as he had spoken."

What a portrait of the Greater Son of Abraham, the Lord Jesus Christ. Way back in the Garden of Eden, God had promised a seed of the woman (typified here by Isaac) who would come to be the Redeemer. But the years slipped by, a hundred, a thousand, two thousand years, and yet the promise remained unfulfilled. Years later, when the hope became dim and the children of Israel, like Abraham, began to wander, the Lord came to repeat the long-delayed promise and caused Isaiah to cry out in Isaiah 7:14,

> . . . Behold, a virgin shall conceive, and bear a son, and shall call his name Immanuel.

And then another seven centuries passed by, and the hope of the coming seed had almost been forgotten by the majority. But God kept His word, and

> . . . when the fulness of the time was come, God sent forth his Son, made of a women, made under the law, To redeem them that were under the law . . . (Galatians 4:4, 5).

A PRACTICAL APPLICATION

We digress here to make a much-needed practical application. One of the lessons we may learn from this account is that God is never in a hurry in working out His plans and purposes, either in the world of nations, or in the life of the individual. Men may fret and fume and rant and rave in their concern about the course of world events, but God has all eternity at His disposal, and works out His plans deliberately, and always on time. We need to learn the lesson of Isaiah 28:

. . . he that believeth shall not make haste (Isaiah 28:16).

We are so apt to become impatient and wonder why God delays so long. We can understand David as he cries out repeatedly, "Make haste to help me, O God" (Psalm 38:22; 40:13; 70:1; etc.). David seems to say, "Hurry up, O Lord! Why does it take You so long?" We too sometimes are tempted to try to hurry up the program of God. We would so gladly lend Him a hand in expediting His program. But God is not in a hurry and His program is running exactly on time, just as He foretold that it would go. So often we become disturbed by conditions in the world, the increase in crime, violence, and wickedness, the rapid spread of communism, the apostasy of the Church, and the threat of a great racial struggle or an atomic conflict. As we behold all these threatening movements we too are tempted to cry, "Make haste, O God," and worse still, we try to help Him out. But all these things have been foretold and are under the complete control of our God. Our one and only business is to preach the Word, *Preach the Word!* We are never to be diverted from this one commission by becoming involved in politics, or continuously preaching against communism and apostasy, by spending our time in bringing about social reform or cleaning up society by the preaching of a social gospel.

As a preacher of the Gospel, I have that one commission, "Preach the Word," and when I depart from this to join the forces which would bring in a man-made Great Society, I am unfaithful to my calling. It is not my business as a preacher to spend my time in civil rights demonstrations, or seeking to bring a Utopia on earth during this dispensation. My one task shall be to preach the Word, not expecting to solve the problems of the nations until Jesus comes. Today God is calling out a remnant, a select minority of believers in response to the preaching of the Word of God. I believe it is a sin for a Christian who knows his Bible to become greatly upset about world conditions as though God were not in control any longer. When the last soul has been saved by the preaching of the Gospel, the Church has been raptured, the nations judged, then Jesus the Prince of Peace will return to set up the *Great Society* as promised throughout the Word of God.

A Word of Caution

So we would issue this word of caution. We must remember that God is still on the throne. He is still in control and everything is running exactly on time and according to His foreordained plan. We would remind you again of the words of Jesus to His disciples in Matthew 24. They had asked Him the question,

> . . . Tell us, when shall these things be? and what shall be the sign of thy coming, and of the end of the world [age]? (Matthew 24:3).

To this question He gives the answer in the balance of the chapter. He does not say that conditions in the world are going to become better and better as the age progresses. Instead He tells the disciples that things will steadily become worse and worse and worse. He warns them against deceivers and false teachers (verse 4). He says that wars and rumors of wars will increase; there shall be famines, pestilences, and earthquakes in divers places. He predicts apostasy increasing toward the end of the age, while racial strife will be rampant on every hand and iniquity shall abound. And now pay special and close attention. Right in the middle of all these predictions He inserts this warning. Notice it carefully:

> . . . *see that ye be not troubled*: for all these things *must* come to pass, but the end is not yet (Matthew 24:6).

All these things *must* come to pass. There is no stopping them. They are planned, predicted and foreknown. All these things *must* come to pass. If this be so, there is nothing we can do to change it. No need for twisting God's arm to make Him change His mind. It is of no use to try to stop God's prophetic train. In due time, He who said He would come, will come, and He will take care of the entire situation. In the meantime we are to *preach the Word*, teach God's people these great truths, alert them to the program of God and the meaning of current events in the light of prophecy, but we are *not to be troubled*. It is of no use to try to hurry God's program. I repeat, for myself, my business is to *preach the Word* and let that do the work. I will not be drawn into political battles, civil rights problems, or international squabbles. I refuse to get excited about the spread of communism, knowing that God Himself will take care of all these things in *His own time* and in *His own way*. The true preacher is never to be drawn away from his one task by trying to stop the conditions around him which the Lord says *must come to pass*. Do you remember the words of our Lord Jesus to one who would be His disciple but *first* had to attend to a little business of his own? When Jesus said to this man, "Follow me," the man said:

> . . . Lord, suffer me *first* to go and bury my father.
> Jesus said unto him, Let the dead bury their dead: but go thou and *preach* the kingdom of God (Luke 9: 59, 60).

There are plenty of people available to bury the dead, but all too few who are available to *preach* the Gospel. The great World Church today has little or no Gospel to preach, but is interested in political reform, social activities, civil rights, international relationships reform, and the building of a Great Society, while the purpose for which Jesus came and to which He sent us is forgotten.

For the Son of man is come to seek and to save that
which was lost (Luke 19:10).

It took me a long while to learn that God did not expect
me to try to convert the world. I recall the day when Paul's
words in I Corinthians 4 opened my eyes to my real responsibility as a preacher of the Gospel:

Moreover it is required in stewards, that a man be
found faithful (I Corinthians 4:2).

If we are faithful in our task, and trust God to keep His
promise, we can live in peace and security in a world filled
with violence.

No, God is never in a hurry in the carrying out of His
program and plans. We may become impatient, fret and
fume at the steady increase of wickedness, threatenings, and
violence, but God says:

. . . see that ye be not troubled: for all these things
must come to pass . . . (Matthew 24:6).

When once we grasp this truth that all that which is hap-
pening is known to God, yes, foreknown by God, then we
can patiently wait for His answer, while we in the meantime are true to His commission:

Go ye, therefore, and teach all nations . . . (Matthew
28:19).

Why does God seemingly delay His answers? Why does
it take Him so long to fulfill His promises? I think we can
find the answer in the birth of Isaac to Abraham and Sarah.
God delayed the birth of Isaac until both Abraham and Sarah
were sterile. God waited unto the powers of nature had
been made an end of. We repeat again the statement that
Abraham's body was *dead* as far as procreation was concerned, and the same was true of Sarah's womb (Romans
4:19). That which is dead must be resurrected and quickened. That which is dead cannot revive itself. It is totally

impossible to do so, and unless a quickening comes from without, nothing but corruption can result. It is a picture of the total depravity of man in the flesh. This is a humbling truth, distasteful to the proud heart of man, and is therefore rejected by the majority.

Before we close this chapter, we would digress somewhat from the main thrust of this message, to make a needed application to the sinner.

The sinner too is spiritually dead. He is not only sick, but *dead*. The state of the natural man is far worse than he imagines himself to be. When man fell and sinned, he died a spiritual death, and was immediately cut off from the source of all life, even God. He is alienated from the life of God (Ephesians 4:18). Until by the grace of God that sinner is brought to the realization that he is dead, and totally unable to do anything for himself, he remains in his state of death. What the sinner needs is *life*, but since he is dead, *life* must come from without. This God did in the case of Abraham and Sarah. He quickened them by His Spirit, restored life to them and they became the parents of the son who was the great type of the Greater Son of whom it is said,

> In him was life; and the life was the light of men (John 1:4).

If you want to be saved, you must abandon all confidence in the flesh, acknowledge you are a hopeless, helpless sinner, dead in trespasses and sins, and need to be saved by a supernatural work of God in the New Birth, whereby the life of God, eternal and everlasting, is imputed to you freely and by grace.

17

A THREE DAYS' JOURNEY

Isaac, the son of Abraham, was supernaturally conceived, and his birth was a foreshadow of the Virgin Birth of Christ. Concerning this son, God had given Abraham many precious promises. God had promised that this son would become the father of many nations, and that through him the whole world would be blessed. God promised that his offspring would be as the sand of the sea for multitude, and the stars of the heaven in number. In due time God kept His promise, and when Abraham was one hundred years old Isaac was born. He grew up in his father's house and then some years later the Lord came and made a most unusual demand of Abraham. He ordered him to take this promised son and offer him for a sacrifice upon Mt. Moriah. Abraham was asked to put to death the son whom God had miraculously given him. Now remember that at the time of this demand, Isaac as yet had no seed; in fact, he wasn't even married. How then could Isaac become the father of many nations if he were to die before he had a child? This was the great test which Abraham faced. We read the record in Genesis 22:

> And it came to pass after these things, that God did tempt [prove] Abraham, and said unto him, . . .
> . . . Take now thy son, thine only son Isaac, whom thou lovest, and get thee into the land of Moriah; and

offer him there for a burnt offering upon one of the mountains which I will tell thee of (Genesis 22:1, 2).

We feel somewhat like Moses when at the burning bush God said to him, "Put off thy shoes from off thy feet, for the place whereon thou standest is holy ground" (Exodus 3:5). Truly Genesis 22 is holy ground to be approached only in deepest reverence, worship and adoration. We have in this chapter one of the clearest figures of Calvary to be found anywhere in Scripture. Together with Psalm 22, Exodus 12 and Isaiah 53, they constitute the highest mountain peaks in the Old Testament, in the progressive revelation of Jesus, the Son of God. We saw Him faintly in the Garden in the first promise of a Redeemer. We saw Him in the lamb slain to provide the bloody skins for our first parents' covering. We saw Him in the Ark of Noah. We saw Him in His supernatural conception in the birth of Isaac. This we studied as we beheld the portrait of Christ in Genesis chapter 21. We urgently recommend that before reading this chapter and the one to follow, that you take time to read carefully and prayerfully Genesis 22, from verse 1 through 14. It will be of immense profit to you.

The Clearest of Types

The chapter is inexhaustible and we shall be able to do little more than to suggest a few of the striking parallels and similarities between the sacrifice of Isaac and the death of Christ upon Calvary. Notice first of all how Isaac is described in this request of God. He says:

> Take now thy son, thine only son Isaac, whom thou lovest . . . (Genesis 22:2).

Immediately it points us to Abraham's Greater Son of whom Isaac is here to be the figure. We recall that well-known verse in John 3:

> For God so loved the world, that he gave his *only begotten Son* . . . (John 3:16).

Like Isaac, Jesus was the "only begotten" of the Father. Then God says, "whom thou lovest." All of Abraham's love was centered upon Isaac; all his hopes were concentrated in him. Jesus too was the well-beloved of the Father, and Luke tells us that at the baptism of Jesus,

> . . . a voice came from heaven, which said, Thou art my beloved Son; in thee I am well pleased (Luke 3:22).

Notice next the place to which Abraham was directed to go as the exact place for the sacrifice of his son. The Lord said,

> . . . get thee into the land of Moriah . . . (Genesis 22:2).

The land of Moriah was the region in Palestine where the city of Jerusalem was built. We are told the exact location by the writer of II Chronicles:

> Then Solomon began to build the house of the LORD at Jerusalem in mount Moriah . . . (II Chronicles 3:1).

In this region was located Mt. Calvary, if indeed the Mt. Moriah does not include Calvary. Notice how specific God was in giving instructions as to the exact place of sacrifice.

Notice in the third place that all this was according to a foreknown, foreordained plan. Abraham was directed to go in faith (not knowing whither he went — Hebrews 11:8). God had it all planned and prepared, just as Jesus, the antitype of Isaac, was the Lamb slain from the foundation of the world.

Another remarkable figure of the Lord Jesus Christ is a prophecy of His burial and sojourn for three days and three nights in physical death in the tomb. Evidently the place from which Abraham was to take his son to Mt. Moriah was a three days' journey. Apparently Abraham was still living in the land of the Philistines in Gerar (Genesis 20:1). There seems to be quite a possibility that Isaac was born and raised in this same country. Mt. Moriah lay some sixty miles northeast of the land of Gerar and would take at least three days to reach. We mention this to show the supernatural, infallible inspiration of the record in order to complete the type of the Lord Jesus Christ in Isaac.

DEAD THREE DAYS

The order to sacrifice and put to death his son came to Abraham three days before the act was to take place. Abraham believed God meant business. There could have been no doubt in his mind about the meaning of the words, "offer him there for a burnt offering." Abraham intended to obey God, and actually slay his son. From the day the command came until he reached Mt. Moriah, three days later, Isaac was potentially dead in the mind of Abraham. There was no doubt, as we see from the preparations he made, that Abraham intended literally to carry out God's word. He took wood for the sacrifice, fire for the offering, and a knife to slay his son (Genesis 22:6). For three days, therefore, Abraham considered his son as good as dead. How clearly it is given to us:

> Then on the third day Abraham lifted up his eyes, and saw the place afar off (Genesis 22:4).

Then after that, as we shall see, he was restored in a figure of the Resurrection. Very likely Paul was thinking of this incident when he says in I Corinthians 15,

> . . . that Christ died for our sins according to the scriptures;
> And that he was buried, and that he rose again the third day *according to the scriptures* (I Corinthians 15: 3, 4).

More about this later. But now notice that this entire transaction was solely between father and son. No other man was to have a part in it. When Abraham reached the mount, he said unto his young men who had accompanied him:

> . . . Abide ye here with the ass; and I and the lad will go yonder and worship, and come again to you (Genesis 22:5).

In the same way, the throngs could follow Jesus from the Garden to the judgment hall and from there to the mount, but when the time for the sacrifice came, all human eyes must be deprived of the sight. What happened between Abraham and Isaac on the mount we may never know here; and so too what transpired between the Father and His Son Jesus Christ during those last three hours of agony we shall never be able to comprehend. It was a transaction between Father and Son. No human eyes were to behold that scene, and so Matthew records, as does Mark:

> Now from the sixth hour there was darkness over all the land unto the ninth hour (Matthew 27:45).

What happened between the Father and the Son during those three dreadful hours we may never know, and we would not tread upon that holy ground. When the final crisis came and the final sacrifice was to be made, God closed the door, snuffed out the lights of Heaven, drew a black curtain across the windows of the sky, hung a crepe on Heaven's door, until finally the culmination came in the ultimate, agonizing cry, "My God, my God, why hast thou forsaken me?"

HE CARRIED THE CROSS

The next verse in Genesis 22 is rich beyond comprehension:

> And Abraham took the wood of the burnt offering, and laid it upon Isaac his son; and he took the fire in his hand, and a knife; and they went both of them together (Genesis 22:6).

Abraham laid the wood for the burnt offering upon Isaac. We surely need to do no more than to quote from John 19,

> And he [Jesus] bearing his cross went forth into a place called the place of a skull, which is called in the Hebrew Golgotha:
> Where they crucified him . . . (John 19:17, 18).

In carrying the wood upon which he was to be sacrificed, Isaac foreshadowed the One who carried His own cross upon which He was to die.

The question arises, how much did Abraham actually know about the typical prophetic meaning of this sacrifice of his son? Was it just an act of blind obedience? or did Abraham understand the meaning of it all? We believe that Abraham understood what all this pointed forward to. Remember that Paul says in Galatians that the Gospel was preached before to Abraham. The amazing thing about the whole transaction is that there is no questioning on the part of Abraham, and no resistance of any kind by the son. The closing sentence of verse 6 is so significant:

> . . . and they went both of them together (Genesis 22:6).

There was perfect agreement; and when Abraham explained the meaning of it all, there was perfect understanding and complete submission on the part of the son. Notice the question Isaac asked his father as they ascended the mountain of sacrifice:

> And Isaac spake unto Abraham his father, and said, My father: and he said, Here am I, my son. And he said, Behold the fire and the wood: but where is the lamb for a burnt offering? (Genesis 22:7).

We would go slow here so you will not miss the point of the answer of faith by Abraham:

> And Abraham said, My son, God will provide himself a lamb for a burnt offering: so they went both of them together (Genesis 22:8).

So they went both of them together. The answer Abraham gave completely satisfied the son. Let us look at the answer again:

> . . . God will provide *himself* a lamb . . .

Notice it does not say, "God will himself provide a lamb," but it says, "God will provide *himself*." Translated freely Abraham says God Himself is going to be the Lamb of sacrifice. While it is true that the Lord also supplied a ram in the bushes as a substitute for Isaac, we believe that the balance of the record looked way beyond the sacrifice of Isaac, and Abraham saw afar off the hill of Calvary where God Himself in the person of His Son would be the Lamb of God sacrificed for us. What else can the words of Hebrews 11 mean, when speaking of Abraham and Sarah:

> Therefore sprang there even of one [Abraham], and him good as dead, so many as the stars of the sky in multitude . . . .
> These all died in faith, not having received the promises, but having seen them *afar off*, and were persuaded of them, and embraced them . . . (Hebrews 11:12, 13).

We shall deal at greater length in our next chapter on the question, "How much did Abraham know about the real significance of the sacrifice of Isaac as a type of the death and the Resurrection of Christ?" Abraham was saved by faith in the promises of God, even though he could not always clearly understand them. At times reason balked at the Word of God, but the record stands:

> By faith Abraham, when he was called to go out into a place which he should after receive for an inheritance, obeyed; and he went out, *not knowing whither he went* (Hebrews 11:8).

Abraham believed God enough to follow His orders, even though he did not know the way, nor where he was going. In the same way we are to trust the promises of God, without question or excuse.

God said it, and when we believe it, that settles it.

18

THE SUBSTITUTE

In our last chapter we left Abraham and his son Isaac alone on Mt. Moriah, both prepared for the burnt-offering which God had commanded. We take up the story from there.

> And they came to the place which God had told him of; and Abraham built an altar there, and laid the wood in order, and bound Isaac his son, and laid him on the altar upon the wood.
>
> And Abraham stretched forth his hand, and took the knife to slay his son (Genesis 22:9, 10).

Everything was done deliberately and without haste. Isaac offered no resistance at all. He could easily have overpowered his aged father. But there was no repining and no refusal. How it carries our minds forward to that scene in Gethsemane hundreds of years later when just before going to the cross, the Saviour cried: "Not my will but thine be done."

The son lies upon the wood, the knife is raised, and Abraham entertained no doubts but that he must bring it down and plunge it into the heart of his son.

BUT WAIT

Just before the fatal stroke falls, God stopped Abraham, and we read:

140

> And the angle of the LORD called unto him out of heaven, and said, Abraham, Abraham: and he said, Here am I.
>
> And he said, Lay not thine hand upon the lad, neither do thou any thing unto him: for now I know that thou fearest God, seeing thou hast not withheld thy son, thine only son from me (Genesis 22:11, 12).

This took Abraham completely by surprise. This was a turn of events he had not expected at all. He fully understood that God meant for him actually to slay his son — and now suddenly God interrupted him.

Here the typology changes and we have an example of a double type. Isaac could be a type of the Lord Jesus only so far and no farther, for Isaac himself needed a substitute who must be slain in his stead. And so the figure changes from Isaac as a picture of Christ, to a ram as a substitute for Isaac:

> And Abraham lifted up his eyes, and looked, and behold behind him a ram caught in a thicket by his horns: and Abraham went and took the ram, and offered him up for a burnt offering in the stead of his son (Genesis 22:13).

IN THE STEAD OF HIS SON

Notice that phrase, "in the stead [or place] of his son." It is a figure of substitution, a picture pointing forward to Christ who was to come in order to die for helpless sinners. Even as a shadow falls short of revealing all the details, features, and colors of the body casting the shadow, so also the types in the Old Testament fall short of fully revealing the person of the Lord Jesus in His work and ministry. We therefore have *double types* as in the case of Isaac. Isaac could be a figure of Christ up to a certain point, and no farther, for Isaac himself needed a Redeemer. When Abraham had done everything but actually and literally slaying his son, God stepped in and altered the picture. Isaac was a sinner himself, and the perfect sacrifice must be an innocent substitute. God had already provided this innocent substitute which could be accepted by God in the stead of Isaac.

So we have here two separate types or figures of the Lord Jesus. Isaac is a figure of Christ, and the ram caught in the bushes also becomes a clear type of the Lord Jesus. All this was in harmony with the previous figures of Christ which we have studied. After Adam had fallen and vainly tried to cover his sin with fig-leaf aprons, the Lord came and revealed the very first principle of atonement by providing an innocent victim to furnish the coats of skins for our first parents. Abel's sacrifice was accepted because he offered a substitute and not the work or sacrifice of himself. This principle of substitutionary atonement can never be violated. We see it in the Passover lamb, in all the offerings commanded by God in the Old Testament, and fully revealed in Christ when He died in our stead. Isaiah says:

> But he was wounded for our transgressions, he was bruised for our iniquities; the chastisement of our peace was upon him; and with his stripes we are healed.
>
> All we like sheep have gone astray; we have turned every one to his own way; and the Lord hath laid on him the iniquity of us all (Isaiah 53:5, 6).

This is substitution — one dying in the place of another. And Paul says in II Corinthians 5:

> For he hath made him to be sin for us, who knew no sin; that we might be made the righteousness of God in him (II Corinthians 5:21).

And the Apostle Peter, bearing testimony to the same inviolable requirement of the substitution of an innocent victim for the guilty one, tells us:

> Who his own self bare our sins in his own body on the tree, that we, being dead to sins, should live unto righteousness . . . (I Peter 2:24).

BACK TO THE MOUNTAIN

But now let us take a still closer look at this transaction on Mt. Moriah where Isaac was spared by the substitution of the ram in the bushes. The record is brief but rich beyond all explanation. We rehearse again the setting. Abraham had bound Isaac on the altar, he had lifted the knife ready to plunge it into his son when the angel of the Lord from Heaven interrupted and revealed the substitutionary ram provided by God.

> And Abraham lifted up his eyes, and looked, and behold behind him a ram caught in a thicket by his horns: and Abraham went and took the ram, and offered him up for a burnt offering in the stead of his son (Genesis 22:13).

Here we have in type and figure the Resurrection of Jesus Christ. After Abraham had considered Isaac dead for three days, he is suddenly restored to him, and kept alive. It was truly like a resurrection from the dead. But Abraham had not expected it to happen in this way at all. He firmly believed he would be called upon to slay his son, and that God would then resurrect Isaac from death. That this was the thought of Abraham is made clear and plain in the record of Hebrews 11. Here is the commentary of the Holy Spirit, almost two thousand years later:

> By faith Abraham, when he was tried, offered up Isaac: and he that had received the promises offered up his only begotten son,
> Of whom it was said, That in Isaac shall thy seed be called (Hebrews 11:17, 18).

Notice that God says Abraham "offered up Isaac: and he that had received the promises offered up his only begotten son." Now we know from the record in Genesis 22 that Abraham did not actually, literally offer up Isaac on the altar, for the angel of the Lord stayed his hand, and revealed to him the substitutionary ram in the thicket behind him. Yet here we have the word of God that "Abraham offered up his only begotten son." Is this a contradiction, a mistake in translation, or what? There is no contradiction. The first two words of verse 17 in Hebrews 11 tell the story, *by faith.*

By Faith

God accepted Abraham's faith and motive for the actual sacrifice. God reckoned it to Abraham as though he had actually slain his son. Had God not intervened, he would have done so, and so Isaac was *potentially* sacrificed by Abraham, and in the mind of God it was so credited. But now we must ask the question, *By faith in what?* What was the content and the basis of this faith which would without murmuring, repining, or argument, give his son to die on an altar? The answer is suggested clearly in the eighteenth verse. Referring to the sacrifice of Isaac, the writer continues:

> . . . in Isaac shall thy seed be called (Genesis 21:12 and Hebrews 11:18).

I wonder if we can trace the logic of Abraham's thinking in this transaction. God had promised him a son some fifty years before. The fulfillment of the promise was delayed by almost thirty years, and then after Abraham and Sarah had both long passed the age of any possibility of having a natural seed, God came to Abraham and repeated his promise. According to nature it was too late. If the promise was to be fulfilled, it would take a miracle, a supernatural conception. And Abraham believed that God was going to perform a miracle to keep His promise, and so we read that,

> . . . Abraham believed God, and it was counted unto him for righteousness (Romans 4:3).

God kept His word. He performed a supernatural miracle, and Isaac was born in God's own time. The miracle had happened. And now the boy is grown up, and God asks

Abraham to slay this son. How was God going to keep His promise that Isaac would become the father of a great nation, if he were to die before he had any offspring? There was only one way in which God could keep His promise, and that was by performing another miracle. And this miracle would be the resurrection of Isaac after he was dead. For, let us remind you, Abraham firmly believed that Isaac would have to die, as evidenced by the elaborate preparations made for the sacrifice as recorded in Genesis 22. Abraham had no idea God would spare Isaac and provide a ram for a substitute. If Isaac, then, were to die, and God was still going to keep His promise, there was only one way—a resurrection. Now we can understand for the first time the willingness of Abraham to obey God. He believed with all his heart that God would keep His promise, and the only way would be by a resurrection. He had trusted God to perform a miracle in the birth of Isaac many years before, and he knew he could trust God to perform another miracle as great or even greater. To sum it all up, Abraham confidently expected to slay his son, in the faith and assurance that, in order to keep His promise concerning Isaac, God would raise him up again from the dead.

Fulfilled in Figure

Abraham offered up his son by faith, and sacrificed the one

> Of whom it was said, That in Isaac shall thy seed be called (Hebrews 11:18).

And now notice the explanation of the whole thing in the verse that follows:

> Accounting that God was able to raise him [Isaac] up, even from the dead; from whence also he received him in a figure [or type] (Hebrews 11:19).

To Abraham the sparing of Isaac was a figure of resurrection. As Abraham looked ahead, he saw the picture of the

Greater Son of Abraham, virgin-born, substitutionarily offered, and supernaturally raised from the dead.

Now back for the conclusion in Genesis 22:

> And Abraham called the name of that place Jehovah-jireh: as it is said to this day, In the mount of the LORD it shall be seen (Genesis 22:14).

Did Abraham understand the meaning of all this? Did he know the meaning of the Gospel which was being preached to him? He certainly did, for he called the name of the place Jehovah-jireh, or *The Lord will provide.* The word *jireh* means "to see ahead." To make provision for anything, we must plan ahead. The word "provide" comes from two Latin words, *pro* and *vide*, or "to look ahead." Abraham called the place: "Jehovah will provide the true Lamb somewhere in the future, of which this experience is only a type." And as Abraham looked ahead, he saw, probably dimly, but he saw the scene on Calvary, and the section ends with a prophecy and an expression of faith:

> . . . In the mount of the LORD it shall be seen (Genesis 22:14).

Yes, Abraham believed God concerning the supernatural birth of a promised son, his substitutionary sacrifice, and his resurrection, and looking ahead saw all of it fulfilled in the Coming One. If there be any doubt left in your minds about Abraham's understanding of these events, we refer you, as we close, to the words of Jesus in John 8:

> Your father Abraham rejoiced to see my day: and he saw it, and was glad (John 8:56).

Now we can understand the persistent, violent attacks by skeptics and unbelievers on the historical record of Genesis. If they could only get rid of these unmistakable portraits of Christ in this Book of Genesis, they would destroy the very Christ Himself, of whom all these men and incidents were but prophetic pointers and identifying figures. And we need not wonder that Abraham was chosen as the father of the faithful, and an example of salvation by trusting the promises of God. God's way has not changed. Today men must be saved the same way, by accepting the record of the Son of God, virgin-born, sacrificially slain, and supernaturally and bodily raised from the dead.

> That if thou shalt confess with thy mouth the Lord Jesus, and shalt believe in thine heart that God hath raised him from the dead, thou shalt be saved (Romans 10:9).

19

THE BRIDEGROOM COMETH

> And Abraham said unto his eldest servant of his house, that ruled over all that he had, Put, I pray thee, thy hand under my thigh:
>
> And I will make thee swear by the LORD, the God of heaven, and the God of the earth, that thou shalt not take a wife unto my son of the daughters of the Canaanites, among whom I dwell:
>
> But thou shalt go unto my country, and to my kindred, and take a wife unto my son Isaac (Genesis 24:2-4).

With the exception of the man Joseph, whose life we hope to study before we conclude this series of portraits of Christ in Genesis, there is none which so perfectly foreshadows and typifies the Lord Jesus Christ as Isaac, the son of Abraham. Given by a supernatural conception, sacrificed on Mt. Moriah, and raised from the dead, Isaac is almost a perfect type of Christ and the story of the Gospel. All this we saw in Genesis 22, which tells us of the sacrifice of Isaac on the mountain. We left Abraham and Isaac there, and now follow closely the balance of the record in Genesis 22. Abraham returned from the mountain, but Isaac was left. Now, of course, Isaac actually came down from the mountain, but the Bible does not say so. As far as the Bible record goes, Isaac stays up in the mountain until he reappears in chapter 24 to meet his bride. We want this to be clear. As far as the record of Genesis is concerned, Isaac is not seen again after his resurrection *until he goes out* into the field to meet Rebekah, his bride. You will not find Isaac's name mentioned once in the balance of chapter 22, or all of 23. Isaac is absent. How clearly it is suggested:

> So Abraham returned unto his young men, and they rose up and went together to Beer-sheba; and Abraham dwelt at Beer-sheba (Genesis 22:19).

But where was Isaac? He is not mentioned. Then follows Genesis 23, recording the death of Sarah. (Sarah represents the nation of Israel.) But in the whole account of the death and burial of Sarah, Isaac is never once mentioned. Surely we can see here the dispensational lesson in the death of Sarah. After Jesus, the Greater Son of Abraham, was slain on Calvary, He disappeared and the nation of Israel is set aside and buried, as it were, without her Messiah. From the record, Isaac did not even attend the funeral of his mother. Jesus, too, the Messiah-antitype of Isaac, was rejected, crucified, and ascended into Heaven. During His absence the nation of Israel is set aside, as represented by the death of Sarah and her burial.

CALLING OF THE BRIDE

Then after Sarah was dead, Abraham sent his servant Eliezer to bring back a bride for Isaac. Probably nowhere in the Bible is there found a picture as complete and beautiful of the calling out of the bride for the Lord Jesus Christ as we have in this type in Genesis 24. Isaac was Abraham's only son. When this son was forty years old, Abraham called his servant, Eliezer, which means "God's helper or guide," to go into a far country and bring back a bride for his son. You recall how he set out into a far country and brought back Rebekah after meeting her at the well in Laban's sheepfold. When this servant of Abraham, who typifies the Holy Spirit, met Rebekah, he showed her the riches of Isaac, and told her the purpose for which he had come, after he entered the home of Bethuel, the father of Rebekah.

Now will you please notice the hard proposition which was put to this young bride. This man, the servant of Abraham, asked her to do three things:

1. She was asked to believe a man she had never met before.
2. She was requested to go to a land from which she was never to return.
3. She was asked to marry a man whom she as yet had never seen.

Here, indeed, was a test of faith, and yet we find from the record that Rebekah decided to go with Eliezer, the servant of Abraham, to wed his son, Isaac. She believed the word of the servant whom Abraham had sent, and upon the evidence of the jewels which he presented as a token to her of the word of this servant, she was willing to set out into this strange land.

Rebekah prepared herself and went with this man to a strange country with which she was totally unfamiliar. She hardly knew in which direction they were going, but she simply trusted her leader who had been sent by the master, Abraham. She believed that he knew the way. And then after a long journey, one day toward evening she lifted up her eyes and saw a man walking in the gloaming, and recognized him, not because she had ever seen him before, but from the faultless description which the servant must have given her all along the way. She recognized *him,* and with a voice filled with emotion, cried out, "What man is this that walketh in the field to meet us?" and the record tells us that the servant said, "It is my master." And you recall the touching incident, how Rebekah, overcome with joy, lighted from the camel and ran to meet him. The blessed scene of greeting is briefly described in these words:

> And Isaac brought her into his mother Sarah's tent, and took Rebekah, and she became his wife; and he loved her . . . (Genesis 24:67).

Surely you have already seen the meaning of this typical and prophetic picture from the life of Abraham and Isaac. God the Father too had an only Son. After He had offered Him up to die on the cross of Calvary, He too sent His servant, the Holy Spirit, represented and typified by Eliezer, into the far country of this old, wicked world to call out a bride, the Church, for His Son, the Lord Jesus. And that Servant was sent out on the day of Pentecost and has been on this journey now for nineteen hundred years, asking men and women to come and become the bride of the Master's Son. The same questions are put to sinners today, which Eliezer expected Rebekah to answer. You remember, they were:

1. Believe a person you have never met before, even the Holy Spirit of God.
2. Go with Him, and allow Him to lead and guide you by faith into a far country from which you will never return as you leave.
3. Be married to a man whom you have never seen before.

This, then, is the simple plan of salvation. It is by faith. We must believe the testimony of the Holy Spirit in this world, or as the Bible puts it, "Whom having not seen, ye love; in whom though now ye see him not, yet believing, ye rejoice with joy unspeakable and full of glory" (I Peter 1:8).

When we believe on Him, and accept the offer of the Son of God, immediately the Servant, the Holy Spirit, opens up the treasures of His grace to our eyes, even as Eliezer opened up the bags of jewels to show the riches of the son to the prospective bride. Then He clothes us with the raiment which the Son has provided, even His sinless righteousness. We set out on a new journey with the Holy Spirit, with only Him and the Bible as our guide. We may not know the next step, but we trust Him, and permit Him to lead. Sometimes the days are dreary and hard, but when the journey seems long, the Holy Spirit tells us more about the One whom we soon are to meet and we take courage and plod on again. And then the Holy Spirit takes some of those precious jewels from the Book of our blessed Master, and with the glittering blessed promises of truth encourages us all along the way. All the way the Servant talks, not of Himself, but only of Him whom we are going to meet. This is what John speaks of in the 16th chapter of his gospel when he says:

> Howbeit when he, the Spirit of truth, is come, he will guide you into all truth: for he shall not speak of himself; but whatsoever he shall hear, that shall he speak: and he will shew you things to come.
> He shall glorify me: for he shall receive of mine, and shall shew it unto you (John 16:13, 14).

This is what the Holy Spirit, typified by the servant of Abraham, does today. He witnesses concerning our coming Lord. He reveals the beauty of Christ in the Book as we journey on by faith.

And then one of these days, as the evening shadows of the closing day of this dispensation come to an end, and the night of the world approaches we will lift up our eyes, and there suddenly in the field of Heaven we shall see Him, and the Spirit within us will answer, "That's Him," and lighting off the camel of our mortality, we shall rise to meet Him in the air, into the open arms of Him whom, though we had never seen Him, we had learned to love. In His eternal tent of many mansions He will bring us, introduce us to His Father and our Father, and the eternal honeymoon of bliss and happiness, where sorrow and pain can never come, shall be ushered in with all of its glory and splendor forever.

We have tried to show you some of the precious jewels of our great Lover, the Lord Jesus Christ, the Shepherd of the sheep. Those of you who know Him will find your hearts beating faster in anticipation of that Blessed Hope. May God grant that those of you who have never said "yes" to the Spirit's call, may now say, "Yes, I will believe His Word. I will turn about and follow that Guide. I will go to wed the Man, who, though I have never seen Him, has won my heart by His great love and the revelation of His kindness through His blessed Word."

The Coming Shepherd

Yes, soon the Chief Shepherd, the Lord Jesus Christ, will come again according to His promise, and then only those who have given heed to the Holy Spirit's call will rise to meet Him, and upon all the rest the dark night of judgment will settle, while we are safe in the house of many mansions prepared for us up there. All the sheep will be in, and the Chief Shepherd will pass out His precious rewards for faithfulness and deck us as a resplendent bride in preparation for His reign upon the earth.

May I ask you, therefore, "Are you ready? Are you looking for His return?" Ah, my friend, if you are not, will you not hearken to the Spirit as He says, "Follow me, and I will lead you to the Father's House"?

> And the Spirit and the bride say, Come. And let him that heareth say, Come. And let him that is athirst come. And whosoever will, let him take the water of life freely (Revelation 22:17).

Beyond question, the journey which Rebekah was asked to make with this man, Eliezer, seemed long and wearisome and endless at times, and yet one can but imagine the joy which must have thrilled her heart when the journey came to an end, and she found that Isaac was far more than all her expectations had ever been able to imagine. He was far more beautiful, far more kind, than she had ever dared to imagine. And, my friend, one of the surprises is going to be, when we meet the Lord Jesus Christ, that we shall cry out, "The half has not been told." It will be so much more wonderful than anything we had even imagined, that our mortal bodies here could not begin to conceive or contain the glory of His blessed Person. And so as we conclude this chapter, again we press upon you the question, Have you listened to His call, and learned to follow Him?

. . . Believe on the Lord Jesus Christ, and thou shalt be saved . . . (Acts 16:31).

20

THREE SHEPHERDS

The Book of Genesis, more frequently attacked by critics and infidels, is far more than an authentic, historical account of the beginnings of the universe and of this earth. Although we believe the brief, unapologetic account of the creation of the universe, the earth and its inhabitants to be a literal, inspired, infallible revelation from God, it is far more than a scientific explanation of things, or a historical account of earth's beginnings. These are merely incidental and secondary to the one plan and purpose of the entire book, as well as the rest of the Bible; namely, the progressive revelation of Jesus Christ, the Son of God and Son of man, Redeemer, and Saviour of men. How old this universe is man will probably never find out, nor would it help him if he did. Just what method and what steps God took to create the world is also of no consequence. The important question for every man is *not*, "Where did I come from?" but "Where am I going?" For this very reason a minimum of attention is devoted in Genesis with the *origin* of things. One verse describes the *beginning* of creation. Two chapters are devoted to the populating of this earth. One chapter is devoted to man's fall and his eternal ruin, and then all the rest of the Book of Genesis, as well as the rest of the Bible, looks to the future and the coming of the Redeemer to restore man into fellowship again. Foolish man, however, has completely ignored the lesson. He is intensely occupied with finding out where he came from, and so he digs into the earth, goes to the bottom of the sea, and now soars out into space, in an effort to find out how it all began, and where we came from. Billions of uncounted dollars are being poured into our space program with the avowed purpose, according to the highest experts, of finding out how it all began. What folly, when they could find out in less than one minute by reading the first chapter of Genesis. Man will never, never, never find a better answer to the question of origin than that given in Genesis 1:1.

The Bible does not waste its time and spend countless billions of dollars on investigating or explaining our origin, but wraps it all up in a few chapters, and then spends the rest of its contents on the *future*, the *eternal future*, and not the non-consequential past. Before you show the slightest interest in the space program, the moon shot, the trip to Mars or Venus, you should settle just one question: "Where am I going? Where will I end up when finally this brief life is over?" Because of the importance of this question, the Book of Genesis is not primarily a book of the beginning of the universe, but a book of the *beginning of the plan of salvation.*

This revelation of the program of salvation is not confined to the New Testament, but begins with the opening verse of Genesis. In direct prophecy and promise, in type and symbol and figure, the Holy Spirit reveals step by step the setting for the coming of the One to whom the entire Old Testament points. Inexhaustible are the types foreshadowing the Coming One. We have seen Adam as a clear type; Abel also; then the Ark as a figure of the Redeemer, and in our last chapters we have seen Jesus Christ the sacrifice for sinners in the history of the birth, death and resurrection of Isaac. Two more men are mentioned at length in the Book of Genesis: Jacob and Joseph, both of them also figures of the One who was to come.

SHEPHERDS IN THE OLD TESTAMENT

There are a number of shepherds in the Old Testament which the Holy Spirit uses as types of the coming Good Shepherd. Among others there are these:

1. Abel, the sacrificing shepherd giving his life and shedding his blood at the hands of his own brother.
2. Jacob, the toiling shepherd, who left his father's house to dwell in a far country, fleeing from the wrath of his brother.
3. Joseph, the exalted shepherd, who, rejected by his brethren, became the saviour of men.
4. Moses, the delivering shepherd.
5. David, the royal, reigning shepherd.

In this series on portraits of Christ in Genesis, we are mainly interested in the three shepherds in this first book of the Bible. We have already studied the type of Abel as the sacrificing shepherd. We come now to Jacob, the loving, toiling shepherd; but before we go into detail, we wish to point out the lessons taught by these various shepherds.

1. Abel was rejected by his brother and put to death. As a result his brother Cain was banished from the land and became a wanderer among the nations. But God in grace supernaturally preserved him against his enemies by putting His mark upon Cain.

In all this we see the story of the rejection of the antitype of Abel, the Lord Jesus, His death at the hands of His brethren, who were then scattered to the four corners of the earth, but supernaturally preserved from extinction for these past centuries, because God has marked this nation as the one which shall exhibit His grace in the future restoration.

2. We see the same thing in the story of Jacob. Hated by his brother, he was driven into exile where he married a bride, and then returned to claim his possession.

3. Joseph, the son of Jacob, was also hated by his brethren, potentially put to death, banished into a far country

where he was exalted to the throne, obtained a Gentile bride, and then after that he returned to redeem his brethren who had sold him.

4. The same story is related about Moses. He too was rejected the first time by his brethren, banished into a far country where he received a Gentile bride, then returned and was accepted by his own at his second coming.

5. David, the royal shepherd, was anointed king, but rejected by his own, forced to flee into the land of the Philistines, there to receive a Gentile bride, and return after the death of Saul, to be accepted and acclaimed by his own nation.

I am sure that in all this we plainly see the record of the One who was rejected by His own the first time He came, and while in rejection is gathering out a Gentile bride, after which He will return to be accepted by His own, and set up the glorious millennial Kingdom.

JACOB AS A TYPE

In the remainder of this chapter we wish to take a brief look at Jacob, the toiling shepherd, as foreshadowing the coming of the Greater Jacob. We shall need the balance of our space to devote to the clearest of all the types in Genesis — Joseph, the son of Jacob. As we take up the different figures of Christ in the Book of Genesis we find that each succeeding one adds some details which were not evident in the previous ones. So we shall find in the story of Jacob some precious revelations, made clear only after we reach the New Testament. Jacob was first of all God's chosen one. God chose him to receive the birthright which naturally had belonged to his elder brother Esau. But Esau forfeited his claim and it passed on to Jacob. Adam, the first man, also had the first natural claim to the dominion of the earth (Genesis 1:26). But the first man forfeited his right to this dominion, and so God sent the Second Man, the last Adam, who is to receive the birthright of the firstborn Son of God.

Notice further that Jacob was hated by his brother Esau, and was caused to flee to a far country in Haran where he toiled as a servant, was taken advantage of, and was shamefully treated. Our Lord Jesus also left His Father's house, and went into a far country to visit His brethren. Here He became a servant and took on Him the form of a man. We read concerning Him in Philippians,

> Who, being in the form of God, thought it not robbery to be equal with God:
> But made himself of no reputation, and took upon him the form of a servant, and was made in the likeness of men (Philippians 2:6, 7).

And now there follows a beautiful dispensational picture. In this house of Laban in the far country were two daughters, Leah and Rachel. Now these two were to become the wives of Jacob. By agreement he was to have Rachel only as his wife, for whom he labored seven long years. But at the end of the seven years he did not receive Rachel, but Leah, her sister, became his first wife. He served seven additional years for Rachel. But Leah became fruitful and gave birth to a family of children while Rachel remained barren and childless. Finally Rachel in her distress and agony began to cry unto the Lord, and when she did, God heard her prayer and she too became the mother of children (Genesis 30:22-24). Jacob had chosen Rachel first, but she was set aside and Leah took her place. I believe we are justified in assuming that Leah represents the Church of this dispensation, and Rachel the nation of Israel, set aside for a season.

I want you to notice what a marvelous picture of dispensational dealing we have in this wonderful record. Leah represents the Church of the Lord Jesus; Rachel, the nation of Israel. He desired her first, but when He came to present Himself to her nineteen hundred years ago, He did not receive her, but she rejected Him, and now Rachel is barren and despised, and Leah, the Church, bearing fruit in the millions of the redeemed who are being brought in during this present dispensation. Israel today as represented by Rachel is an empty vine, while the Church is fulfilling the purposes of God. But Israel like Rachel, according to Scripture, shall yet bear. There is a time coming when she too shall become fruitful and bring forth Josephs and Benjamins, the beloved ones and the sons of the Lord's own right hand. It is of this future restoration of the nation of Israel and her fruitfulness and her dominion over the earth, that Isaiah speaks in Isaiah 54:

> Sing, O barren, thou that didst not bear; break forth into singing, and cry aloud, thou that didst not travail with child: for more are the children of the desolate than the children of the married wife, saith the LORD (Isaiah 54:1).

And a little farther on we hear the Lord speaking in this strain:

> For thy Maker is thine husband; the LORD of hosts is his name; and thy Redeemer the Holy One of Israel; The God of the whole earth shall he be called.
>
> For the LORD hath called thee as a woman forsaken and grieved in spirit, and a wife of youth, when thou wast refused, saith thy God.
>
> But for a small moment have I forsaken thee; but with great mercies will I gather thee.
>
> In a little wrath I hid my face from thee for a moment; but with everlasting kindness will I have mercy on thee, saith the LORD thy Redeemer (Isaiah 54:5-8).

Do you not see the glorious picture of the future of the nation? The time is coming when Leah, the Church, will be taken up, and God will again begin to deal with Israel; they shall look upon Him whom they have pierced and accept Him. He will turn their captivity and gather them from all the nations whither they have been driven, and they shall be settled in their own land and become the great and wonderful heritage of the Lord and the instrument by which millions upon millions will be turned to Jehovah, their Lord and their God.

Now as we continue the story of Jacob as the toiling and loving shepherd, notice that on the way back to his father's house he brought both wives home in triumph. That is what Jacob did, and so on the way home he received a new name. His name was changed from Jacob to Israel, and the name "Israel" means "the prince of God." We are told in the Book of the Revelation that when Jesus Christ comes back again with His Bride to bless Israel and all the earth, He has a Name which no man knows but Himself. This, beloved, is God's program for the Good Shepherd of Israel and the Church. He came once and was rejected by the ones He came to save, and, setting them aside for a time, He is now calling out a bride, the Church of His love. After she is called out, He will return again to Israel who the first time rejected Him, and be their Deliverer and their Saviour and their Lord. Then shall He establish the Kingdom on earth, and every knee shall bow to Him, and every tongue confess that Jesus Christ is Lord to the glory of God the Father.

21

FOUR STEPS IN REDEMPTION

There are exactly four men who dominate the last thirty-nine chapters of Genesis. The first eleven chapters of Genesis span a period of 2,000 years of man's history. That is all God wanted us to know about the first two millenniums of man's sojourn on earth. And it was a sordid history of sin, rebellion and judgment, ending in the Flood. Then after the record of the Flood, God began a brand new section by calling out of idolatrous heathendom one man by the name of Abram. The knowledge of the true God had well-nigh disappeared from the earth, and God, in order to reveal His plan of salvation, separated one man from the rest of humanity, and through his son Isaac and grandson Jacob separated to Himself a peculiar, called-out, covenant nation, Israel. This nation was to become God's peculiar possession, the repository of divine revelation, the vessel in which the true worship of Jehovah was to be preserved, and out of whom in the fullness of time the promised seed of Genesis 3:15 was to be born. As we have pointed out previously, these four men whose lives span only four centuries occupy the center of the stage in the last thirty-nine chapters of Genesis, and represent the four successive steps in God's program of redemption. Abraham is the great example of divine, sovereign election by grace; Isaac is the example of selective calling; Jacob the great example of salvation by grace and grace alone, and justification by faith. Joseph is the great picture of glorification. Beginning with divine election and culminating in glorification, God revealed in type His plan which Paul must have had in mind when he wrote:

> . . . whom he did *predestinate*, them he also *called*: and whom he called, them he also *justified*: and whom he justified, them he also *glorified* (Romans 8:30).

All this we have touched on in preceding chapters. We come now to the most complete type of the Lord Jesus Christ in the Book of Genesis. His name was Joseph, the son of Jacob. Although the story of Joseph is familiar to anyone who has ever attended a few sessions in Sunday school, the record is inexhaustibly rich. There are far more similarities and parallels showing Joseph as a type of Christ than probably any other person or event in the Old Testament. We shall have time to point out only a few, in the hope that it will stimulate you to give personal attention to this intriguing and profitable study. There are over one hundred incidents and details in the study of the history of Joseph which point beyond any question to the One of whom he is such a clear type. Many more similarities I am sure can be found by the student of Scripture who will study chapters 37 to 50 of the Book of Genesis.

Among the innumerable figures of Christ in the history of Joseph we therefore mention only a few taken more or less at random. Notice first the fact that Joseph had *two* names, one given to him when he was born and another name when he was exalted to the throne of Egypt. The name given to Joseph by his father means "adding to," or "increasing." As the last Adam and the Second Man, Jesus is indeed the Great *Adder*. The first Adam was the great subtractor; the last Adam is the great multiplier. Speaking of Himself, Jesus says in John 12,

> . . . Except a corn of wheat fall into the ground and die, it abideth alone: but if it die, it bringeth forth much fruit (John 12:24).

Joseph is the equivalent of the name Jesus — His human name given to Him by His parents under instruction by the Holy Spirit. As the Son of man, He was rejected by His brethren just as Joseph was, sold for thirty pieces of silver, cast into the pit of death, and sent into exile. But after many fierce and cruel trials, this Joseph was finally exalted to the right hand of Pharaoh in Egypt, and received a new name, not the name of rejection but exaltation. Moses tells us in Genesis 41:

> And Pharaoh took off his ring from his hand, and put it upon Joseph's hand . . .
> And he made him to ride in the second chariot which he had; and they cried before him, Bow the knee: and he made him ruler over all the land of Egypt.
> And Pharaoh called Joseph's name Zaphnath-paaneah . . . (Genesis 41:42-45).

Zaphnath-paaneah means "the revealer of secrets." It is his name of authority, and points forward to the Second Coming of Jesus Christ. When Christ came the first time in humiliation and shame, to be rejected by His brethren, His name was Jesus, but when He comes again to reign in power and glory He will receive a new name. The Apostle John describes this Second Coming of Christ in glory and power in Revelation 19:

> And I saw heaven opened, and behold a white horse; and he that sat upon him was called Faithful and True, and in righteousness he doth judge and make war.
> His eyes were as a flame of fire, and on his head were many crowns; and he had a name written, that no man knew, but he himself (Revelation 19:11, 12).

What this new name of Jesus will be, we may never learn here below, but I am sure it will correspond to the new name of Joseph, Zaphnath-paaneah, the revealer of secrets, for then everything hidden shall be revealed, and all the secrets of the hearts of men shall be made known.

By occupation Joseph was a shepherd, and one of the

great types of the coming Good Shepherd. Joseph was hated by his brethren because he exposed the evil of their hearts. When he was just a lad of seventeen, he visited his brethren who were tending their sheep in Shechem. Joseph saw the conduct and wickedness of his brothers, and reported it to his father (Genesis 37:2). For this he was hated all the more. Our Lord Jesus too when He came to this world was hated because He revealed man's wickedness and testified against them. He says in John 7,

> The world cannot hate you; but me it hateth, *because*
> *I testify of it, that the works thereof are evil* (John 7:7).

Moreover, Joseph was the well-beloved of the father. We read significantly in Genesis 37:

> Now Israel loved Joseph more than all his children,
> because he was the son of his old age; and he made
> him a coat of many colours (Genesis 37:3).

Jesus too was the well-beloved of the Father. He too was the Son of the Father's old age, even from eternity, and one of His names is *the Ancient of Days.*

JOSEPH THE DREAMER

Joseph as a type of Christ was not only a shepherd, but he prefigured Christ as the Prophet, the foreteller of the future, and especially his own future. Already Joseph was hated by his brethren because he testified to his father concerning their wicked deeds, and because he was his father's favorite son and was honored by wearing a coat of many colors, which distinguished him from the rest of them. But he caused them to hate him still more when he came with his prophetic dreams. The dreams Joseph related to his brethren were a source of jealousy and anger to them. First Joseph saw his brethren as sheaves of wheat in the field bowing down to him, a prophetic vision which was soon to be fulfilled in Egypt. Then in a second dream he saw the sun and the moon and the eleven stars making obeisance to him. These words, prophetic as they were, incensed his brethren against him. It was his words to which they took exception. They hated him not only because of *who* he was (his father's beloved son) but because of what he said. In Genesis 37:8 we have this:

> . . . And they hated him yet the more for his dreams, and for his words.

What a prediction of the hatred of Christ's enemies. They too hated Him because of what He claimed Himself to be. John says,

> Therefore the Jews sought the more to kill him, because he . . . said also that God was his Father, making himself equal with God (John 5:18).

But they also hated Him because of what He said. He said,

> But now ye seek to kill me, a man that hath told you the truth, which I have heard of God . . . (John 8:40).

In connection with the two separate dreams which Joseph related to his brethren, we call your attention to the two separate areas in which the dreams are seen. The first was on earth. Joseph saw sheaves of grain in the field bowing down to him. The field is the world, and this dream speaks of earthly sovereignty. The second dream was in the heavens as he saw the sun, moon and eleven stars making obeisance to him. Here we have sovereignty in the heavens. Here Joseph points forward to the Lord Jesus who will some day reign as sovereign Lord and King, even as He is today Lord in Heaven. The sheaves bowing may well speak of His earthly Kingdom, the promised Davidic Kingdom, and the sun, moon and stars, His heavenly people, the Church, and the redeemed from all ages.

He Came to His Own

We come now to events in Joseph's life whose typical applications are so clear that none with open, unprejudiced

mind can miss them. Joseph, the beloved of the Father, was
sent by the father to visit his brethren and present to them
his gift (Genesis 37:12). The father was deeply interested
in the welfare of the brethren, and sought their good (Genesis 37:14). Joseph went to Shechem where his brothers had
last been heard of, but found them not. Shechem means fellowship, and the brothers had moved to Dothan which means
law. Here Joseph found them in the land of the law. But
when they saw him coming, they were filled with hatred
and said:

> . . . Behold, this dreamer cometh (Genesis 37:19).

They conjured up a false plot to get rid of him and cast
him into a pit without water, while they were to decide what
to do with him. And then they had a break (as they thought),
for a band of Ishmaelites came passing by, and Joseph's
brothers sold him as a slave to the Ishmaelites for twenty
pieces of silver, and he was exiled into Egypt.

Before we follow Joseph any farther, we must show the
striking similarity between the treatment of Joseph by his
brethren, and the abuse of Jesus by His brethren. The story,
though familiar, bears repeating:

> And it came to pass, when Joseph was come unto his
> brethren, that they stript Joseph out of his coat, his coat
> of many colours that was on him;   .
> And they took him, and cast him into a pit: and the
> pit was empty, there was no water in it (Genesis 37:
> 23, 24).

We pause here to call attention to the coat of many colors
mentioned so frequently in the narrative. It evidently was
a very expensive, valuable coat, given to him by his father
to mark him off as a specially distinguished figure. This
coat was evidently a *seamless robe,* woven in one piece with
opening only at the top and bottom. It had to be put on
over the head or stepped into, having no opening on the

sides, front or back. This is certainly indicated by the language in our Scripture. Notice it carefully:

> . . . they stript Joseph *out of his coat*, . . . (Genesis 37:23).

It does not say they took the coat off, or stript it from Joseph, but they stript him *out of his coat*. It is not incidental or accidental that in the record of Jesus' trial we read the same story. After the scribes and Pharisees, His brethren, had tried to kill Him but found the pit dry, they turned Him over to the Gentiles, but not before stripping Him and retaining the seamless coat of many colors. In John 19 we read of the soldiers and Jesus:

> Then the soldiers, when they had crucified Jesus, took his garments, and made four parts, to every soldier a part; and also his coat: now the coat was without seam, woven from the top throughout.
> They said therefore among themselves, Let us not rend it, but cast lots for it, whose it shall be: that the scripture might be fulfilled, which saith, They parted my raiment among them, and for my vesture they did cast lots . . . (John 19:23, 24).

It is no mere coincidence that both Joseph, the type, and Jesus, the antitype, wore the distinguishing garment of a father's special love, a seamless garment.

After they had stripped Joseph and cast him into the pit, we read a very interesting insertion:

> And they sat down to eat bread . . . (Genesis 37:25).

While their brother was in the pit, the place of potential death, they were completely unconcerned and went right on eating their lunch. It was the same with the ones who crucified our Lord. After He had been nailed to the tree we read Matthew's account, which is almost a paraphrase of the conduct of the brothers of Joseph, in Matthew 27,

> And they crucified him, and parted his garments, casting lots: . . .

And sitting down they watched him there (Matthew 27:35, 36).

Space compels us to draw this chapter to a close, and, the Lord willing and tarrying, we continue the typology of Joseph in our next installment. We have barely touched the surface of the rich, typical meaning, for it is inexhaustible.

I am sure that you must have felt a sickening revulsion at the treatment of Joseph by his brethren, and an even greater revulsion at the wholly illegal, unjustified murder of the Son of God. But do you realize, my friend, that it was our sins, yours and mine, which nailed Him to the cross. We are as sinners represented by the brethren of Joseph and the mob that led the Son of God to the hill of Calvary. And yet He is the very One who now stands ready to forgive and save. What marvelous grace!

22

JOSEPH, THE DELIVERER

For purity of character, for steadfastness under trial, for unswerving perseverance in following the right, there is no Old Testament character to compare with Joseph, the favorite son of Jacob. At the age of seventeen he was sold into slavery in Egypt, was subjected to the most severe temptation, and yet he persevered, and by the age of thirty had become the prime minister of Egypt. However, our chief interest in Joseph in these messages is the typology of his history as a figure of the Greater Saviour of the world, the Lord Jesus Christ. In the preceding chapters we pointed out a number of striking parallels in the life of Joseph and that of Jesus, similarities so evident that they are unmistakable. We saw Joseph's two names, one given him at birth, and another given him when he was exalted to the throne. By occupation he was a shepherd, type of the Chief Shepherd of the Church. He was hated without a cause, delivered into the hands of the Gentiles, sold for twenty pieces of silver, and potentially put to death. He was the well-beloved of his father. He wore a distinctive robe of many colors. Joseph was sent by his father to his brethren with a message, and to bring a report, but they despised him. Jesus also was sent by the Father to His brethren, but:

He was in the world, and the world was made by him, and the world knew him not.

He came unto his own, and his own received him not
(John 1:10, 11).

Joseph was stripped of his raiment and cast into the pit to
die, but came out of the place of death alive. He was sent
into Egypt and became a servant. He was falsely accused by
Potiphar's wife and cast into prison. He attempted no defense, and in prison he was numbered with the transgressors.
While in the prison of rejection, he became the saviour of the
king's butler but the judge of the king's baker. The butler
was set free, and in due time mentioned Joseph's name to
the king who had had a terrifying, mystifying dream. Joseph was called and interpreted the dream for Pharaoh, and
received his new name, Zaphnath-paaneah. He was exalted
to the throne of Egypt, and became the saviour of the world
in the great famine. While exalted on high he was given
a Gentile bride. And then follows the account of his brethren
in Canaan facing starvation with their father Jacob. In their
desperation, having heard that there was corn in Egypt, the
ten brothers journeyed to Egypt to buy corn. They were
recognized by Joseph as his brethren, while at the same time
he was unknown to them. At the hands of Joseph, these
brethren were severely punished, and their past crime of
selling their brother was brought vividly to mind. Before
he would identify himself they must first be brought to their
knees in confession of their guilt and crime of the potential
murder of their little brother. The narrative is interesting
beyond description. In Genesis 42 we read:

> And Joseph was the governor over the land, and he it
> was that sold to all the people of the land; and Joseph's
> brethren came, and bowed down themselves before him
> with their faces to the earth.
> And Joseph saw his brethren, and he knew them, but
> made himself strange unto them, and spake roughly unto
> them; and he said unto them, Whence come ye? And
> they said, From the land of Canaan to buy food.
> And Joseph knew his brethren, but they knew not
> him.

And Joseph remembered the dreams which he dreamed of them, and said unto them, Ye are spies; to see the nakedness of the land ye are come (Genesis 42: 6-9).

Then Joseph really turned on the heat. "The chickens had come to roost." They were finding out that "whatsoever a man soweth, that shall he also reap." Joseph made these ten brothers tell all about their family, and especially Joseph's youngest brother, Benjamin. He put them in prison for three days, and then let them go, but demanded that one of the brothers be detained in Egypt until they would bring Benjamin back with them to prove that they were not spies.

Now if you suppose that Joseph was mean and revengeful in his action, you are mistaken. He had a purpose and a plan in it all, and it was to become a picture of the future dealing of the Messiah and His people of Israel in the latter days. The plan began to work. Conviction overcame them, and I hear them huddled together, and saying:

. . . We are verily guilty concerning our brother [Joseph], in that we saw the anguish of his soul, when he besought us, and we would not hear; therefore is this distress come upon us.

And Reuben answered them, saying, Spake I not unto you, saying, Do not sin against the child; and ye would not hear? therefore, behold, also his blood is required.

And they knew not that Joseph understood them; for he spake unto them by an interpreter.

And he turned himself about from them, and wept; and returned to them again, and communed with them, and took from them Simeon, and bound him before their eyes.

Then Joseph commanded to fill their sacks with corn, and to restore every man's money into his sack, and to give them provision for the way: and thus did he unto them (Genesis 42:21-26).

They returned home, but soon they ran out of food and had to return. This time they dared not return without tak-

ing Benjamin along to prove they had not been lying. Over
the bitter protest of father Jacob, Benjamin was taken along.
And then the real trial came, for when the brothers were
ready to return, the silver cup of Joseph was slipped into
the top of Benjamin's sack. They were scarcely gone when
upon Joseph's orders they were overtaken, accused of having
stolen the precious cup, and returned to the palace. The
sacks of grain were carefully searched, and, to the utter dis-
may of the brethren, it was found in Benjamin's sack. The
consternation among the sons of Jacob was indescribable.
It meant that Benjamin was accused of theft, and would
have to be detained as a slave in Egypt. While the story
is familiar, we feel that reading the record once more will
be profitable. After the brethren had been ordered back
to the palace and accused of stealing the silver cup, Joseph
said unto them:

> . . . What deed is this that ye have done? wot ye not
> that such a man as I can certainly divine?
> And Judah said, What shall we say unto my lord?
> what shall we speak? or how shall we clear ourselves?
> . . . behold, we are my lord's servants, both we, and he
> also with whom the cup is found.
> And he [Joseph] said, God forbid that I should do so:
> but the man in whose hand the cup is found, he shall
> be my servant; and as for you, get you up in peace unto
> your father.
> Then Judah came near unto him, and said, Oh my
> lord, let thy servant, I pray thee, speak a word in my
> lord's ears, and let not thine anger burn against thy
> servant: for thou art even as Pharaoh (Genesis 44:15-
> 18).

Then follows the touching, heart-rending plea of Judah
in behalf of his aged father, and he said that if Benjamin did
not return Jacob would drop dead. Now we come to the
real crux of the whole matter. Judah now recalled the incident in the field when Joseph was sold, and he was forced
to rehearse the whole pitiful, sad story. Here are the words

of Jacob, when they took Benjamin away, as told by Judah, now, to Joseph:

> And thy servant my father said unto us, Ye know that my wife bare me two sons:
> And the one [Joseph — still unrecognized by them] went out from me . . . and I saw him not since [over twenty years].
> And if ye take this also from me, and mischief befall him, ye shall bring down my gray hairs with sorrow to the grave.
> It shall come to pass, when he seeth [us returning without the lad] . . . *he will die* . . . (Genesis 44:27-29, 31).

> Then Joseph could not refrain himself before all them . . . (Genesis 45:1).

This was all Joseph could stand. His purpose had been accomplished. He had wrung from them a confession of their guilt and sin. He had seen his dreams come true of the sheaves bowing down to him and the sun, moon, and stars making obeisance. Who can imagine the agonizing moments of these brethren before Joseph, as he caused all their evil past to rise up before them. He saw their agony as the past came back to haunt them. They recalled how they had cast him into the pit, closed their ears to his cry, lied to their father, and thought that it would never be revealed. But the "mills grind slow, but they grind exceeding small." Everything that needed to be accomplished in the purpose of God had been done, and the time was here to reveal himself to them as their brother Joseph. We shall read it as it is written, lest we spoil it.

> Then Joseph could not refrain himself before all them that stood by him; and he cried, Cause every man to go out from me. And there stood no man with him, while Joseph made himself known unto his brethren.
> And he wept aloud: and the Egyptians and the house of Pharaoh heard.

> And Joseph said unto his brethren, I *am Joseph*; doth my father yet live? And his brethren could not answer him; for they were troubled at his presence (Genesis 45:1-3).

And then Joseph freely forgave them, and we come to the climax:

> And he [Joseph] fell upon his brother Benjamin's neck, and wept; and Benjamin wept upon his neck.
> Moreover *he kissed all his brethren,* and wept upon them: and after that his brethren talked with him (Genesis 45:14, 15).

The rest of the story you know. Jacob and all his family were brought from Canaan to dwell in the richest part of Egypt. These despised Hebrews were favored above all the people because *their brother was on the throne.*

This is indeed the climax of the typology of Joseph, when he freely forgave his brethren who had sold him into Egypt. Now why have we rehearsed this story at length when it is so familiar to all? Mainly because of its dispensational application to the nation of Israel. We cannot fail to see the portrait of Jesus in Joseph's whole history as the Saviour of mankind. But there is another interpretation too often overlooked. Joseph and his brethren are a type of God's great program for the nation of Israel.

JESUS THEIR MESSIAH

Joseph is not only a type of the Saviour of the world, but the *Messiah* and the King of Israel. Jesus typified by Joseph was the Father's well-beloved Son. In the fullness of time He sent Him into the field of the world to seek His brethren. He found the nation of Israel in the land of Dothan, the land of the law. But they rejected Him, and sold Him for thirty pieces of silver into the hands of the Gentiles. While in rejection by them He sits on the right hand of the King of the universe, receives a Gentile bride, awaiting the time of the Great Tribulation and the day of Jacob's trouble (represented by the seven years of famine). After a dispensation of plenty since the Messiah was rejected, there will follow the seven years of earth's greatest sorrow, and the brunt of it will be borne by the nation of Israel. It is indeed called the

TIME OF JACOB'S TROUBLE

Speaking of that great day of the Lord, the Tribulation period, lasting seven years and of which the famine in Egypt was a type, Jeremiah says:

> Alas! for that day is great, so that none is like it: it is even the time of Jacob's trouble, but he shall be saved out of it (Jeremiah 30:7).

Joseph did not forget the evil of his brethren, and meted out their just punishment to them in their agony during the famine; so, too, Israel's sin must be confessed, she must bear her punishment, and then she shall be saved. This is the reason Joseph did not wreak revenge upon his brethren by refusing them bread, but neither did he overlook their sin and he made them smart for it. In Acts 7 Stephen, in rehearsing the story of Joseph, tells us:

> But when Jacob heard that there was corn in Egypt, he sent out our fathers first.
> And at the *second time* Joseph was made known unto his brethren . . . (Acts 7:12, 13).

Yes, at the *second time* he is made known to them. The first time "he came unto his own, but his own received him not." The world's last great climactic time of trouble and tribulation prefigured by the seven years' famine in Egypt is drawing very, very near. The Church will be with her Lord on the throne, and then the vials of God's wrath will be poured out with vengeance and a time of trouble ensue, so great that unless those days were shortened, there should no flesh be saved. Why didn't Joseph make himself known the first time, instead of permitting them a time of agony and sorrow without precedent? Because his brethren must be brought to their knees before him and confess their guilt. The Bible predicts this time of Israel's agony and their deliverance. Jeremiah says:

> For mine eyes are upon all their ways: they are not hid from my face, neither is their iniquity hid from mine eyes.
> And [but] first I will recompense their iniquity and their sin double . . . (Jeremiah 16:17, 18).

And after they have been almost annihilated and destroyed, the Lord will make Himself known to Israel, even as Joseph did to his brethren, and

> I will cut off the chariot from Ephraim, and the horse from Jerusalem, and the battle bow shall be cut off: and he shall speak peace unto the heathen: and his dominion shall be from sea even to sea, and from the river even to the ends of the earth (Zechariah 9:10).

It is then that the Greater Joseph shall reveal Himself to His brethren, the sons of Jacob, and forgive their sins and iniquities, and, like Joseph, overcome them with love and compassion and forgiveness. Of this truly Isaiah sings in Isaiah 40:

> Comfort ye, comfort ye my people, saith your God.
> Speak ye comfortably to Jerusalem, and cry unto her, that her warfare is accomplished, that her iniquity is pardoned: for she hath received of the Lord's hand double for all her sins (Isaiah 40:1, 2).

Then He will lead them into the choicest of the land and exalt them above all the nations of the earth. As we see the signs of the times multiplying and the indications of Israel's great day of trouble, we would cry out:

> O Lord Jesus, how long, how long,
> Ere we shout the glad song:
> Christ returneth, Hallelujah!
> Hallelujah, Amen.

23

THE PERFECT ANTITYPE

The story of Joseph is beyond a doubt the clearest type of the personal ministry and exaltation of Christ to be found anywhere in the Old Testament. The record relating the story of Joseph might well be the basis for a library full of books instead of a few brief chapters. We have followed the history of Joseph up to the time he was made known to his brethren, as they sought to buy corn in Egypt. In this message we want to look at just one aspect of the history, the revelation of the sovereign, overruling grace of God. It is told by Joseph himself in a most dramatic way in Genesis 45:4-8,

> And Joseph said unto his brethren, Come near to me, I pray you. And they came near. And he said, I am Joseph your brother, whom ye sold into Egypt.
> Now therefore be not grieved, nor angry with yourselves, that ye sold me hither: for God did send me before you to preserve life.
> For these two years hath the famine been in the land: and yet there are five years, in the which there shall neither be earing nor harvest.
> And God sent me before you to preserve you a posterity in the earth, and to save your lives by a great deliverance.
> So now it was not you that sent me hither, but God:

and he hath made me a father to Pharaoh, and lord of
all his house, and a ruler thoughout all the land of
Egypt.

What an example of the all-wise, overruling providence
of God making even the wrath of man to praise Him. Years
before, these brethren of Joseph with wicked intent had sold
him into Egypt, never expecting to see him again. The guilt
was great, their sin indescribable, and yet God permitted all
this to come about with an eye to the future welfare of the
very murderers of their brother. God permits man to sin in
order that He may work out His own sovereign plan and
will. Now if this statement be challenged by anyone, let me
remind you that God is sovereign in all His actions. Go
with me to the Garden of Eden, and see there the exhibition
of God's mysterious ways. From a beginningless eternity
God was all alone, by Himself. Before there were moon or
sun or stars, planets or constellations, God already was. He
did not have to create the universe. He did not have to
create the earth on which we dwell. He did not have to
create man in His own image, and place him on this earth.
But for reasons known only to Himself, and with some final
goal in view, He created the universe, and in this universe
one little earth, and placed on this one little earth, one little
created being called man. God knew before He created man
that he would turn out to be a rebel and sinner. Yet knowing this before, He created man nevertheless. He could have
created a man who could not sin, for God is sovereign. Yet
He created a being who could sin, and whom He knew
would sin, and did not stop him. After God created a man
who could sin, God could have kept him from sinning, for
God is absolutely sovereign in all He does. But instead of
preventing man from sinning, which He was able to do, He
nevertheless *permitted* man to fail and come under the penalty of death. Now we may argue the matter forever, but
we shall never be able to *deny* the fact that God permits

evil to come in order that out of it may come some greater revelation of Himself.

We shall never fully understand these things, but some things we can see faintly. Had Adam not sinned, there would have been no need of redemption. Without Adam's sin, we would never have known the plan of salvation, would never have known the love of God for a sinner, or the grace that could save the vilest sinner. This does not explain everything, but we can see that God made man's sin the occasion for the revelation of Himself in redemption, for the sending of His Son into the world to die for sinners. Were it not for sin, Christ would never have come, there would have been no Incarnation, no Bible, no gospel hymn-books, and all the other blessings made possible by the revelation of God to poor, lost sinners in the person of the Lord Jesus Christ. Now someone may say that man therefore was justified in sinning, but this is not so. Man is guilty, worthy of death, without excuse of any kind. We would not minimize the gravity of man's sin, but we would exalt the majesty of the love and grace of our God, who could in response to man's sin reveal such a marvelous plan of redemption. We shall not delve deeper into this mystery of mysteries, but the fact remains that God made man's helpless, hopeless, fallen state the occasion for the revelation and exhibition of His love and grace, and all this is personified in the Lord Jesus Christ. Paul answers the whole question when he says in Romans 5:20,

> . . . But where sin abounded, grace did much more abound.

The Case of Joseph

If you have any objections to these statements, let me take you back to the history of Joseph, that outstanding type of the Lord Jesus Christ. In Genesis 45 we read that Joseph recognized the fact that God had used the sin of his brethren in selling him into slavery as the means of carrying out His program of deliverance, not only for his brethren, but the nations round about. He said to his brethren:

> And God sent me before you to preserve you a posterity in the earth, and to save your lives by a great deliverance.
> So now it was not you that sent me hither, *but God* . . . (Genesis 45:7, 8).

Now this did not excuse these wicked brethren, and Joseph surely made them to smart for their sin. They were just as guilty as ever, but now looking back, Joseph could see God's hand and purpose in *permitting* these wicked brothers potentially to put him to death. This is a hard truth to accept, and it was a difficult thing for the brethren of Joseph to accept. Joseph had brought them into Egypt and dealt graciously with them, but still they were fearful that some day they would be punished by Joseph. Finally father Jacob died and now the brethren became more apprehensive.

> And when Joseph's brethren saw that their father was dead, they said, Joseph will peradventure hate us, and will certainly requite us all the evil which we did unto him.
> . . . Forgive, I pray thee now, the trespass of thy brethren, and their sin; for they did unto thee evil: and now, we pray thee, forgive the trespass of the servants . . . (Genesis 50:15, 17).

But their fears were all in vain. They were indeed guilty, but they had been fully forgiven, and then notice the answer of Joseph:

> But as for you, ye thought evil against me; but God meant it unto good, to bring to pass, as it is this day, to save much people alive.
> . . . And he comforted them, and spake kindly unto them (Genesis 50:20, 21).

What a wonderful picture of the grace of God. God could permit these wicked men to sell their brother, lie to their father, and then afterward use this very act, this dastardly sin, to become the means of salvation for the very ones who were guilty. And the deliverance was complete. Can we find a more beautiful portrait of the Lord Jesus Christ in the entire Bible than Joseph weeping with his brethren who had rejected him, and then reading:

> . . . And he comforted them, and spake kindly unto them (Genesis 50:21).

Yes, these brethren meant it for evil, but God could take their sin and make it the means of ultimately saving them alive, bringing them into the land of plenty, and reuniting them with the brother whom they had rejected. Surely in all this we see the clear portrait of the Altogether Lovely One. It is indeed comforting to know that when we sin and err and stumble, the Lord not only stands ready to forgive and pardon, but even shows us afterward that He knew it all beforehand and made plans to bring blessing out of the tragedy. This does not excuse our sin, but it exalts His marvelous grace. As we look back over our own experiences we too can trace the hand of divine Providence and sovereign grace in some of the darkest moments and deepest trials of our life. There were times when everything was against us, when there was no way out, and we could only sink in dark despair. But now the years have passed, and we begin to see the design in all of this which the Lord permitted to come upon us. We now can see that some of the most trying experiences of life which drove us to the brink of despair were God's way of preparing something better for us. Yes, and as we look back we can see where God used our mistakes and blunders to teach us the most valuable lessons, and lead us into avenues of service which we would never have known except for these. This, we repeat, does not excuse our mistakes and sin, nor cause us to say, "Let us therefore sin that grace may abound," but it does magnify and exalt the infinite, limitless, loving grace and kindness of our forgiving Saviour.

> God moves in a mysterious way
> His wonders to perform;
> He plants His footsteps in the sea,
> And rides upon the storm.

> Blind unbelief is sure to err
> And scan His work in vain;
> God is His own interpreter
> And He will make it plain.

> Ye fearful saints, fresh courage take;
> The clouds ye so much dread
> Are big with mercy and shall break
> In blessings on your head.

For the greatest demonstration of the grace of God in response to man's sin, we must of necessity go to Calvary. So come with me, and follow the One of whom Joseph was only a shadow. He was the perfect, sinless Son of God who did not have to come into this sinful world to redeem us. God was not obligated to send His Son. God had spoken: "The day thou eatest thereof, thou shalt surely die." Man disobeyed, and God had a perfect right to damn Adam on the spot and banish him forever. Justice demanded it. But instead, God planned a redemption, and in the fullness of time Jesus came, was rejected by the very ones He came to seek. They captured Him like a criminal, subjected Him to an illegal trial by night, inflicted the most savage brutality upon Him, struck Him in the face, plucked out His beard, spit upon Him, stripped Him naked, scourged Him, and then led Him up the hill of Calvary to die. Now *listen!* That Man was the innocent Son of God. He had done no evil. So here we remind you again that a sovereign God could have stopped this entire, unspeakable murder of His innocent Son. We repeat, God could have prevented the suffering and murder of His Son, for He is sovereign, and the Son was innocent. Why then did not God step in and stop that mad mob? But instead God *permitted it,* and made no move to interfere. As He hung upon the cross, the cruel oriental sun beating upon His fevered, naked body, a howling mob of sadistic savages taunted Him and challenged Him to come down from the cross. We feel like crying out, "O God, where are You? O God, why do You permit this infamy to continue? O God, this is Your lovely Son who hangs there in agony, and He is innocent, and His tormentors are guilty sinners. O God, do something! *Do* something!" But there is no answer; instead He plunges His Son in a God-forsaken darkness as He snuffs out the sun and stars, draws down the curtains of Heaven, as the Son now cries:

> . . . Eli, Eli, lama sabachthani? that is to say, My God, my God, why hast thou forsaken me? (Matthew 27:46).

Once more we ask, "O God, what's the matter with You? How can You keep silent? Why don't You send fire from Heaven and consume this mob? Why don't You send a deluge of brimstone and sweep them all into Hell? It is what they deserve. You have a right to damn them forever. O God, give us an answer."

Listen! Listen!

There is an answer. God can do something bigger than send those murderers all to Hell. Yes, God has a greater plan in mind. He could permit these murderers to put to death His Son, and then *make the death of His Son the only means of saving those murderers from Hell.* God could take the murder of His Son, and make it the means of saving the murderers.

Stand in Awe and Wonder

This is the story of Joseph, who said to his brethren:

> But as for you, ye thought evil against me; but God meant it unto good, to bring to pass, as it is this day, to save much people alive (Genesis 50:20).

The shadow was fulfilled at Calvary.

> Marvelous grace of our loving Lord,
> Grace that exceeds our sin and our guilt;
> Yonder on Calvary's mount outpoured,
> There where the blood of the Lamb was spilt.
>
> Grace, grace, God's grace,
> Grace that will pardon and cleanse within;
> Grace, grace, God's grace,
> Grace that is greater than all our sin.

AN AUTHOR'S FAREWELL

It was with a great deal of anticipation that I began many months ago the preparation of material for this latest volume, *Portraits of Christ in Genesis.* I had no idea of the wealth of material that would be uncovered, or even the inability to begin to deal with the important matters superficially. As I finished the writing of the last chapter I experienced a certain sense of utter frustration and failure at not having been able to go more thoroughly into some of the depths of the marvelous revelation in this unique and unusual book of the Old Testament. After all my years of Bible study I was utterly amazed at the amount of material and the wealth of revelation found in this Book, of which in past studies I had caught glimpses, but never fully realized. And even with this increased knowledge of the Word of God in Genesis, I recognize the fact that we have merely dipped our toes into the vast expanse of the infinite ocean of the relevation of God. The Bible is a Book of the progressive revelation of the Person of the Lord Jesus Christ.

Recently Genesis has been under special attack by the enemies of the Lord Jesus Christ. This is not hard to understand when we realize that probably nowhere do we find more clear, definite, unmistakable pictures of the Person of Christ, than we do in the Book of Genesis, and so the attack upon the book is really an attack upon the Person, in an effort to destroy Him and His authority.

As we come to the end of our studies, I want to make a few practical applications which I have personally experienced, and which have been a blessing to my own heart. First of all, I have appreciated more than ever before the greatness of the God with whom we have to do. In the Book of Genesis we find clearly delineated the five basic attributes of the Person of God, which set Him apart as the One God, and beside whom there is no other. These five attributes of God which *must* be true if He is God, are:

1. The Sovereignty of God.
2. The Omniscience of God.
3. The Omnipotence of God.
4. The Omnipresence of God.
5. The Omnirighteousness or justice of Almighty God.

Each of these attributes is absolutely indispensable and essential if we are to have a God in whom we can trust, and in whom we can place the eternal destiny of our souls.

First of all, God must be sovereign in *all* that He does; for if He be not sovereign, then there could be someone higher than He, and this would leave us always in doubt as to His ability to see us through completely unto the end. The Bible begins with the statement of the sovereignty of God. No other book possibly could begin in this way: "In the beginning God." This is the peculiar, unique method with which God introduces the revelation concerning Himself. He makes no excuses; He makes no explanation; He does not stoop to the credulity of man in order to give a reason for what He is doing, but makes the categorical statement, "In the beginning God created." There it is. You can take it, or you can leave it. And upon the acceptance or rejection of this original opening statement concerning the sovereignty of God depends everything which follows. Once we accept this statement, "In the beginning God created," there is nothing which follows in the entire Book which we cannot accept by faith. The One who was able to create out of nothing a universe, the vastness of which we are just beginning to appreciate today, certainly would not be limited in anything that He did as far as having a fish swallow a man, or walking on the water, or healing the sick, or raising the dead, or cleansing a leper. These are mere trivialities compared with the tremendous statement with which the Bible opens, "In the beginning God created."

I would like to place great emphasis upon this point, for once we have accepted by faith the dictum that in the beginning an All-wise, All-sovereign God created the heavens and the earth, and was not responsible to explain to His creature how or why He did it, we have the secret to faith in anything else which God may say. The miracles recorded in the Bible as performed by God through men, or through Jesus Christ, or throught the Apostles, are mere, trivial incidentals as compared with the stupendous miracle of being able to create out of nothing a universe as vast as we are beginning to appreciate now. I therefore would make the bold statement that perhaps the most important verse in the entire Bible is Genesis 1:1, because everything depends upon this. Once we accept "In the beginning God created the heaven and the earth," nothing is impossible any more. We can accept anything from there on. However, if we reject this statement that in the beginning God created the heavens and the earth, we cannot place any confidence or faith in any other statement which follows in the Word of God. It is in this verse, Genesis 1:1, where faith begins, and infidelity stumbles. It is the key verse for the study of the entire Word of God. If we do not accept the sovereignty of God, we have no God who is worthy of trust and confidence, and we are left in a maze of uncertainty and doubt.

The second attribute which is absolutely essential to our proper faith in God, and which is clearly revealed in the

Word of God is the attribute of omniscience. By omniscience we merely mean that God knows everything from the beginning to the end. He marks the sparrow's fall. The hairs of our head are numbered, and there is not a single thing that happens in the world, not a leaf that stirs, not a blade of grass that falls, which is not known by Him, and not only known by Him, but known beforehand, and planned by Him as well. Now it is impossible for us to comprehend a statement of that kind, and we are not expected to, but we are expected to believe it, just as we accept the sovereignty of God, and His power in creation. It is essential that we not only believe in a sovereign God, but that we believe in an omniscient God; for if God does not know everything beforehand, He might be taken by surprise, and something might occur of which He was not cognizant, and we might be left without a proper and a reliable guide. Omniscience, therefore, a perfect knowledge of God concerning all of our life, past, present and future, is absolutely essential if we are to put our faith and trust for a timeless eternity in such a God.

In the third place, a God whom we can respect and rely upon completely must not only be sovereign and omniscient, but He must be omnipotent. This is the theological term for all-powerful. If God be not all-powerful, then it stands to reason that there could be someone who is more powerful than He, and then when we put our reliance in Him, we might come to the place where He Himself suffers defeat, and we would be defeated with Him. God must be all-powerful. This of course is implied in His sovereignty in the very first verse of the Bible. We have all of the attributes of God already suggested. Certainly we see sovereignty in the first verse, "In the beginning God created." We also see omniscience, for only God could plan a universe as great as this in which we live and have it all perfect as it came from His hand. After God had created the universe, He did not have to wait until some of the "bugs" were taken out, some corrections were made. It was not a matter of trial and error; it was not a matter of improvement or gradually developing the universe, but everything was absolutely perfect from the time that He created it, so that there had to be no alterations or changes or additions, either in the materials or in the laws which govern the universe today. When we look at man's efforts, we see the difference. Think, for instance, back fifty years, of the original, old automobiles which we drove in those days, and then the things in which we are driving about today. We see how man has to profit by his mistakes, and gradually gather new knowledge, and make changes and alterations, and then never reach perfection. But not so with God, for He is not only sovereign and omniscient, knowing all things beforehand, but omnipotent. So He could create a universe in the beginning; and the moment it came forth from His hand it was complete and perfect, never to need any alterations, additions or subtractions.

The fourth attribute of God which we feel must be true, or we cannot trust Him completely, is His omnipresence, by which we merely mean that He is everywhere present. He fills all the universe and beyond, and "whither shall I flee from His presence?" The psalmist enumerates all the places where he might possibly be hidden from the all-seeing eye of God, and finally he comes to the conclusion that no matter where he might hide, God would be able to find him. How foolish man is that he tries to hide from God, and by various and devious means seeks to fool God, as though the Lord would not be able to find him. What a comfort it is to our hearts to know that He is omnipresent! When we find ourselves in a difficult situation, He is right there at hand, for even the Lord Jesus Christ who is God, has promised us, "Lo, I am with you alway, even unto the end of the world." If we were to find ourselves in a difficult situation, and then would have to wait for God to arrive from some other place, even at great speed, it might jeopardize our very safety. So the omnipresence of God becomes an absolute necessity for our faith.

Finally, we have coined the term, the "omnirighteousness of God." God must be just, He must be righteous in all of His doings, or we cannot trust Him. Unless God be honest and righteous and just in everything that He does, He cannot be worthy of our trust and of our confidence.

And so we have enumerated these five attributes of God, all of which are clearly illustrated in the first book of the Bible, the Book of Genesis.

Before we close this discussion we want to make one further practical application, and that is that in the providence of God and in the omniscience of God, it is His rule that suffering leads to victory, and there is nothing worth-while attaining in life which does not have some price attached to it. While salvation is full and free, for the believer there is a price tag for every blessing which he expects to receive from the hand of God. This is following in the footsteps of the Master Sufferer Himself, the Lord Jesus Christ, who Himself was not made perfect without sufferings.

As I lay my pen aside, and I do so with absolute and full and complete confidence in the sovereignty, the omniscience, the omnipresence, the omnipotence, and the omnirighteousness of a holy God, I dare to commit to Him the keeping of my soul without fear. I do not feel that I need to defend One who is sovereign and omnipotent. I do not feel that I need to present any proof for the existence of One who is already omniscient and all-wise and all-righteous. He only needs to be preached. In these days in which we are living, there is a tendency and a temptation, I must admit, that we shall be drawn away by attempts to defend the Word of God against the vicious attacks of the enemy on every hand, and yet we have only one commission: *preach the*

Word. It is not our business to go out to prove the Bible to be the Word of God, or to defend an almighty and omnipotent God. We have but one commission which is entrusted to our care, and that is to declare the revelation of God in the person of the Lord Jesus Christ. For this reason we have published this volume, *Portraits of Christ in Genesis,* and trust it will be used of the Lord for His glory and for the profit of His children.